ARTISANS AND FAIR TRADE

CRAFTING DEVELOPMENT

ARTISANS AND FAIR TRADE

CRAFTING DEVELOPMENT

Mary A. Littrell and Marsha A. Dickson

Kumarian Press
An Imprint of Stylus Publishing

Artisans and Fair Trade: Crafting Development

Published in 2010 in the United States of America by Kumarian Press
22883 Quicksilver Drive, Sterling, VA 20166, USA.

The authors gratefully acknowledge the generous funding provided by the Earthwatch Institute and the Rockefeller Foundation for this research. In addition, our academic departments at Colorado State University, Iowa State University, Kansas State University, and the University of Delaware provided graduate research assistants, release time for research, and travel support.

The text of this book is set in 11/13 Garamond

Editing and book design by Aptara

The paper used in this publication meets the minimum requirements of the American National Standard for Information Sciences—Permanence of Paper for printed Library Materials, ANSI Z39.48–1984

Library of Congress Cataloging-in-Publication Data
Littrell, Mary Ann.
    Artisans and fair trade : crafting development / Mary A. Littrell and Marsha A. Dickson.
        p. cm.
    Includes bibliographical references and index.
    ISBN 978-1-56549-321-6 (pbk. : alk. paper) – ISBN 978-1-56549-322-3 (cloth : alk. paper)
    1. Handicraft industries–India.   2. Artisans–India–Economic conditions.
3. Economic development–India.   4. Social responsibility of business.
5. International trade–Moral and ethical aspects.   I. Dickson, Marsha Ann.
II. Title.
    HD9999.H363I46 2010
    331.7'94–dc22
                                                                              2010017335

Contents

List of Illustrations

Figures

Tables

List of Abbreviations

ATA	Aid to Artisans
ATO	Alternative Trading Organizations
BMN	basic minimum need
CACTUS	Care and Concern Toward Us
CMT	cut, make and trim
CSR	corporate social responsibility
FLA	Fair Labor Association
FLO	Fairtrade Labelling Organizations International
FWF	Fair Wear Foundation
HDI	United Nations Human Development Index
IFAT	International Federation of Alternative Trade
ILO	International Labour Organization
NGO	nongovernmental organization
NIFT	National Institute of Fashion Technology
SAI	Social Accountability International
SEWA	Self Employed Women's Association
SFTMS	Sustainable Fair Trade Management System
SHARE	Support the Handicapped's Rehabilitation Effort
WARE	Women Artisans Rehabilitation Enterprise
WFTO	World Fair Trade Organization

Acknowledgments

We offer our deep appreciation to Pushpika Freitas, founder and President of MarketPlace: Handwork of India. From our first meeting at a Fair Trade Federation conference in 1992, Pushpika has served as inspiration to us in learning about fair trade and artisans' lives. Throughout our research, Pushpika served as our champion, sounding board, and guide. We are deeply grateful to her for opening MarketPlace to our intense scrutiny. While Pushpika and others at Market-Place offered crucial insights for our analysis, the final interpretations are our own. We hope that this book does justice to what Pushpika and the artisans of MarketPlace have accomplished.

From the beginning of our research, the MarketPlace artisans believed in the importance of telling their MarketPlace story. For many artisans, the interviews brought back memories about difficult times in their lives. However, we hope that the interviews also allowed the artisans to reflect positively on what they have accomplished for their children, households, and personal lives. We are humbled by the strength that the artisans conveyed throughout the project and will always be grateful for their willingness to share their life stories. In recognition of the artisans' commitment to the project, the royalties from the publication of this book will be contributed to SHARE's social development programs for the artisans and their families.

Two MarketPlace leaders in India truly made our research possible through their superb management skills. Fatima Merchant, Director of SHARE, provided invaluable direction in organizing and setting up the on-site framework for the daily activities in Mumbai. Devi Nair, Associate Director of SHARE, made all interview appointments and was with us on a daily basis as she attended to the needs of the volunteers and cheerfully kept us focused on our work. We will always be grateful to Fatima and Devi for their dedication to our project.

Across the two years of interviews in India, twenty-four Earthwatch volunteers joined us as research assistants. We are appreciative of their genuine interest in the artisans of MarketPlace, their lives, and their work. Volunteers were conscientious about taking detailed notes and in obtaining stories from the artisans that provided richness to the analysis. Our volunteers arrived in Mumbai from four countries.

Team 1
Sally Campbell	United States
Jocelyn Chua	United States
Barbara Jones	United States
Brad Jones	United States
Kevin Jones	United States
Laura Kastner	United States
Julie Mills	Australia
Mary Lee Winer	United States

Team 2
Elise Boer	Canada
Michael Boer	Canada
Beth Brewster	Great Britain
Sue DiPuccio	United States
Joan Frank	United States
Elizabeth Redman	Great Britain

Team 3
Nancy Appleton	United States
Carol Bath	Australia
Melody Beier	United States
Sophie Browne	Australia
Janell Gehrman	United States
Susan Hall	United States
Gisa Indebaum	United States
Karol Jensen	United States
Sarah Oliver	Great Britain
Ilene Winnikur	United States
Melody Snyder (research assistant)	United States
Susan Strawn (research assistant)	United States

As we think back over the time with our volunteers, a number of highlights emerge. For all of us, we experienced the great privilege of visiting the women's houses. What pride the women displayed as they shared with us the space they called home! For nearly all the women, this was the first time they had hosted a foreign visitor. As the interviews evolved, the artisans talked openly about their successes, hardships, and daily challenges. Prior to each research team's departure, a lively afternoon party of games and songs with the artisans concluded our time in Mumbai. Repeatedly, the artisans shared with us how much they liked talking with the volunteers. For the researchers and volunteers, these positive feelings are mutual!

A project such as this involves substantial financial support. We gratefully acknowledge the Earthwatch Institute in Maynard, MA, for funding our field research trips to Mumbai. We hope that our resulting book helps accomplish Earthwatch's goal of bringing "science to life for people concerned about the Earth's future." In addition to the Earthwatch grant, we each received support from our respective universities, which, at the time of the research, were Iowa State University and Kansas State University. Additional support has been offered by our current institutions, Colorado State University, and the University of Delaware. Finally, we acknowledge the Rockefeller Foundation, which awarded us funding for a month of writing time as resident scholars at the Rockefeller Foundation Bellagio Center in Bellagio, Italy. The critique of our work from fellow Rockefeller resident scholars was insightful in shaping the book.

From the day that we first contacted him, our editor Jim Lance enthusiastically encouraged us to tell the MarketPlace story of fair trade and artisan development. Along the way, he suggested additional scholarship in which to ground our analysis and answered our many questions. We offer our sincere appreciation to Jim for recognizing and supporting scholarly analysis of fair trade and its impacts on artisans' lives.

Across the many years of our research with MarketPlace, our husbands, John Littrell and Scott Dickson, have supported us, encouraged us, fed us, and taken care of the home fronts during our extended trips to India. Thank you for believing in the importance of our work.

CHAPTER 1

Artisan Enterprise, Fair Trade, and Business Social Responsibility and Accountability

Corporate responsibility has typically been defined by the corporation, on its own terms, and reported by it without external audits.
Corporate accountability means the corporation is held to account for
commitments made. Corporate accountability, in these terms, is CSR
with teeth.

–Michael E. Conroy, Author of *Branded! How the "Certification
Revolution" Is Transforming Global Corporations.*

In the next few years, the World Fair Trade Organization will clarify
standards and markers that help consumers make judgments about fair
trade. Reducing fair trade to a single measurement [fair price] is not
good enough.

–Paul Myers, President of World Fair Trade
Organization (WFTO).

MarketPlace is about giving women a chance to prove themselves,
make a difference and bring about change that they want to bring
about—change that will benefit their daughters and sons and the society
at large.

–Pushpika Freitas, Founder of MarketPlace.

During our first week at MarketPlace: Handwork of India, a fair
trade enterprise in Mumbai, India, Monisha[1] invites us to meet
her family. Leaving the noisy, sunlit street outside the MarketPlace
office, we traverse a labyrinth of dark lanes to her home in the Golibar
slum. Water from community taps adds slickness to the uneven surfaces
underfoot. Closing in on us from either side, monochromatic gray, single-
room homes, joined by common walls, line the narrow pathways. Thin metal

stairs, precariously attached to an outside wall, lead to second-floor rooms added for rental income. Fabric curtains flap in the doorways; occasionally, we catch a glimpse of family life through the small windows facing the lanes. Colorfully adorned women nod to us as they sit in their doorways, cleaning vegetables; the aromas of pungent curries fill the air. Rounding a corner, we collide with two sisters on their way to purchase lentils for their family's evening meal. Children dart from side lanes, busy playing street games. Heat diffuses into the pathway from steam irons used by tailors who are lodged into tiny shopfronts of their homes. Periodically, we note a block of latrines that accommodates hundreds of households. This dense community with its commercial activity, temples, and mosques serves as home to Monisha and other MarketPlace artisans.

Monisha's two daughters, twelve-year-old Asha and fifteen-year-old Rima, greet us at the doorway of their 10-by-10-ft home.[2] Their eighteen-year-old brother is away attending his afternoon classes in the twelfth standard. Walls are freshly painted a pastel blue in the family's immaculate home. Monisha's stacks of shiny cooking vessels ascend one wall; a bed and a storage cupboard line the adjacent wall. In a corner, a television, covered with a protective towel, stands ready for viewing. Asha and Rima invite us to sit on the floor. Asha tells about her classes and how much she likes to study; she wants to be a teacher. Her sister proudly shows us drawings of *mehendi* painting, decorative designs applied to women's hands and feet for weddings, produced during a class for children of MarketPlace artisans. Both girls ask where we are from and what life is like in America. Monisha joins us, offering aromatic cups of chai. She describes her struggles as a widow and imparts with great pride that, despite disputes with her in-laws, the home is now in her name. When we asked Monisha how her neighbors treat her, she notes that some neighbors are jealous because she has gained so much confidence from her MarketPlace work. However, they also see that she is a good woman and treats her children well. Asha and Rima suggest that we next visit their mother's MarketPlace workshop.

Rounding a dimly lit corner, the chatter of women announces a workshop entrance. On the ground floor, the 10-by-10-ft workshop overflows with piles of fabrics, three sewing machines, and a small cutting table. Upstairs, twenty women sit cross-legged on the floor, intent on their embroidery. Despite the cramped conditions, the workshop is spotless and airy, with over-head fans providing relief from Mumbai's premonsoon heat. After removing our shoes, finding a place on the floor amid the knee-to-knee assembly of women, and receiving more chai, we begin our conversation. Women inquire whether it is acceptable for them to continue their embroidery while we talk. The previous week, a management consultant from Great Britain had introduced the concept of value-added time; the women are eager to apply the concept as we converse.

The women hunger for stories about our lives as American women— "What are your love marriages like?" "How many years did you go to school for your job?" "Why do you eat meat if there is such a cholesterol problem in the US?" When guessing each other's ages, all of us erupt in gales of laughter but then settle down to probing inquiries about what it means to be "old" in our two countries. Across our exchange, we came away with the intense impression that a window to the world has opened for MarketPlace women; they are reaching out to be part of something larger.

Monisha is one of over 300 artisans, nearly all women, who compose MarketPlace: Handwork of India (MarketPlace), a fair trade organization located at the edge of the Golibar slum in Mumbai, India. Fair trade enterprises are grounded in a set of socially responsible practices that include paying a fair wage in the local context, offering equitable employment opportunities among workers, providing healthy and safe working conditions, promoting environmental sustainability, offering business and technical training, and building long-term trade relations (WFTO, *Ten Standards of Fair Trade* 2009). In our 1999 book, *Social Responsibility in the Global Market: Fair Trade of Cultural Products,* we proposed that "fair trade fosters empowerment and improved quality of life for artisan producers through an integrated and sustained system of trade partnerships among producers, retailers, and consumers" (5). While we and others involved in documenting fair trade practices had substantial anecdotal evidence to support this statement, comprehensive empirical assessment was nonexistent for documenting social and economic impacts.

This book explores the fair trade claim of empowerment and improved quality of life among artisans who have had the opportunity to work under the model to which fair trade is committed. Through interviews with artisans, managers, and founders, we conducted a systematic socioeconomic audit of MarketPlace artisan employment. The audit supported our objective of illuminating in both quantitative and qualitative ways how fair trade work impacts the lives of artisans. As such *Artisans and Fair Trade* offers the first in-depth, empirical critique of social and economic impacts from fair trade artisan work.

MarketPlace: Handwork of India

Founded in 1986, MarketPlace grew from roots in a modest sewing project for impoverished women, initiated by Pushpika Freitas and Lalita Monteiro in Mumbai, India. As two of six sisters, they grew up in a family of modest means but with a value for education and progressive attitudes toward their daughters. As Pushpika explained, "At age twenty-two, I had no concept that women had no control over their lives. I was more like someone who had grown up in Evanston [Illinois], where I currently live, than in Mumbai." Immersed in her mother's involvement as a social worker with leprosy patients, Pushpika started conversing with the women.

> I saw so many women working so hard to keep the family going and having a really hard time making ends meet for their families. They were ready to do anything. I didn't sit down and think, "How am I going to solve this problem? How am I going to affect people's lives?" It was more, "Let's just try something." We started with three women. They had no income at the time. One was a widow. The others had husbands who did not work. All had small children.

Initially, women sewed patchwork quilts, drawing inspiration from household practices of recycling clothing for younger family members and for sewing bed quilts. The women's well-honed embroidery and sewing skills, learned while growing up in their Indian families, served as the critical resource for income generation (Littrell and Dickson 1999). From the outset, cultural practices of recycling were firmly embedded in production. As Pushpika explains,

> Nothing, and I really mean nothing, is thrown out in India. Newspapers are made into bags, and these bags are used to pack fruits and vegetables at the local markets. Old bottles are sold, never thrown out. In rural areas, where firewood is used for cooking, the ashes are used to wash the cooking utensils and the coir in the coconut is used to scrub the utensils. When I visit India, I always take back sturdy plastic bags because I know they will be used for many, many years.

Today, MarketPlace artisans produce Western-style apparel, accessories, jewelry, and household textiles with strong aesthetic links to India. Two hallmarks distinguish MarketPlace textile products with their intense colors and dramatic motifs. All fabrics incorporate hand production, through dyeing, printing, or weaving. Each product is then embellished with hand embroidery that highlights fabric motifs and introduces striking points of emphasis. Because artisans often work under a single overhead light bulb in their homes, embroidery purposefully follows easy-to-see design lines in the printed or dyed fabrics.

As a business enterprise, MarketPlace was founded as a single production unit. However, as the organization grew, it became top-heavy with supervisors. Today, seven independent workshops offer employment to anywhere from twenty to seventy workers and are organized such that much of the machine sewing of garments is done on-site, with women carrying out the embroidery work in their homes. Under these circumstances, women workers capitalize on opportunities to intersperse their apparel work with household responsibilities and care of young children across a day.

MarketPlace's Indian-inspired products are marketed in the United States through specialty retail stores, a mail-order catalog, and the Internet (see Figure 1.1). MarketPlace catalogs are unique for their "global dialogue" sections centered on promotional themes chosen by the women, such as "Life's Journeys" or "The Power of Identity."

As a fair trade organization, MarketPlace has operated from its inception with a dual focus on generating income in the profit-driven global marketplace and developing capabilities for the empowerment of low-income artisans. Two organizational arms, MarketPlace Bombay and SHARE (Support the Handicapped's Rehabilitation Effort), provide direction to the business and social thrusts, respectively.[3] In addition to technical and business training, MarketPlace artisans are privy to a variety of social programs offered through SHARE. Artisans actively participate in regular discussions of women's health, legal rights, gender issues, and intergenerational dynamics. At monthly "global dialogue" meetings, promotional themes for the catalogs are identified and artisans contribute stories about daily life in India to share with US customers. In addition to the discussion groups, each production unit carries out a social action project addressing a community problem in their slum.

As MarketPlace has evolved, the enterprise mirrors Nash's (2000) assessment that successful artisan ventures incorporate a broad rather than a narrow range of goals. MarketPlace's efforts toward economic and social development fit within the larger Indian context where government leaders have called for training programs that encourage self-efficacy, creativity, and problem solving (Dana 2000). Such programs are intended to counter long-standing cultural norms of external loci of control, acceptance of destiny, and passivity.

Fair Trade Approach to Business

Since the inception of fair trade in the 1950s, the movement has evolved through four waves of growth and change. Initially, fair trade businesses emerged after World War II in Great Britain, the Netherlands, Germany,

Figure 1.1 Examples of MarketPlace catalog covers.

Figure 1.1 (*Continued*)

Canada, and the United States. Two catalyst groups sparked the formative years of North American fair trade. In the late 1940s and 50s, Mennonite and Church of the Brethren missionaries, returning from abroad, brought artisan goods for church and home-based sales. Revenue from the sales was returned to artisans in desperate need of income in the communities where the missionaries worked around the world. In the 1950s, fair trade emerged in the United Kingdom with Oxfam beginning to sell fair trade handicrafts (Conroy 2007). These early fair trade businesses were described as alternative trading organizations (ATOs) because they aimed to provide desperately poor artisan producers access to international markets (Littrell and Dickson 1999; Nicholls and Opal 2005). As we describe the first two waves of fair trade, we retain the phrase "ATOs." However, by the 1980s, the term "fair trade" replaced alternative trade; accordingly, we describe the movement as fair trade through the ensuing waves of change.

From its inception, alternative trade was a development activity that utilized market mechanisms to reduce poverty (Nicholls and Opal 2005). Alternative trade provided new opportunities for small producers who would otherwise not be able to participate in the global economy due to lack of political and economic power. An overarching goal was to resolve inequitable trade relations (Murray and Raynolds 2007; Raynolds and Wilkinson 2007). ATOs were engaged in direct trading relationships with small produc-ers in developing countries, maintaining close ties that were established through long-term partnerships between ATOs and their artisan producers. Personal visits were made by ATO leaders to identify producer groups that could benefit from fair trade practices that included empowering work-ers through capacity-building projects that expanded capabilities for life and work. ATOs also made commitments to return as much money as possible to the artisans, rather than as little as possible as was typical in conventional trade relationships (Littrell and Dickson 1999; Nicholls and Opal 2005).

In alternative trade, "producer and consumer are brought closer together by the information flows that serve to bridge the spatial distance that sepa-rates them" (Nicholls and Opal 2005, 153). ATOs used hangtags, brochures, and in-store forums to educate consumers about conditions the produc-ers faced in their daily lives. Through the information ATOs shared with consumers about life conditions and stories of how lives were improved from sales of producers' products, strong relationships of solidarity were created between consumers and the producers (Littrell and Dickson 1999; Mukherjee and Reed 2009; Nicholls and Opal 2005). Consumers' trust in the alternative trade system was developed through the close relationships ATOs fostered (Nicholls and Opal 2005). Nicholls and Opal (2005) describe the important foundation that ATOs provided for the fair trade movement through their pioneering work:

> ATOs represent the origins of fair trade, and as such, are an essential part of the story of the development of the fair trade system, its certification, and impressive growth (80) . . . [ATOs] effectively established a market for fair trade in the North and played an important role in raising awareness of trade injustice. (230)

From the 1960s through the 1980s, early ATOs were joined by a second wave of businesses with similar focus on development, including Market-Place and Pueblo to People in the United States, and Traidcraft in the United Kingdom. In this period, social activists, concerned about poverty and what they perceived to be increasing gaps between the rich and the poor, traveled abroad, established contacts with artisans as a sign of solidarity to their plight, and offered to sell their goods upon return home.[4] These new entrants to alternative trade also offered handcrafted goods, but extended their marketing through a new range of catalogs and world-focused retail shops (Littrell and Dickson 1999; Nicholls and Opal 2005). From these dual origins, fair trade sales expanded significantly. As an example, revenue for Ten Thousand Villages, the largest North American fair trade business, grew from $6.1 million in 1995 to $24 million at the end of the 2008-2009 fiscal year.

As the numbers of organizations involved in fair trade grew, they began collaborating in order to benefit from each other's knowledge and experiences conducting fair trade. In the United States, the Fair Trade Federation was formed in 1994 and served as a collaborative forum among North American ATOs and their producer organizations. In Europe, the International Federation of Alternative Trade (IFAT) was formed in 1989 as a global network of ATOs (Conroy 2007).

A third wave of fair trade during the 1980s and 1990s brought an increasing focus on food products and initial participation of big retailers. This period marked a turning point in the development of fair trade, particularly for agricultural commodities. The fair trade coffee business, Equal Exchange, was started in the United States in 1986. Sympathetic European retailers that wanted to sell a small portion of fair trade products, particularly coffee, in their stores joined the fair trade movement. Because these large retailers would sell fair trade food products alongside their traditionally traded products, there was need for a label that would distinguish which products were fairly traded (Conroy 2007).

During the late 1980s and early 1990s, a series of national labeling initiatives was created, starting with one developed by the Max Havelar

Foundation in the Netherlands. Early product certification efforts focused on further empowering small producers; the standards were aligned with original fair trade goals (Reed 2009). By 1995, several independent labeling initiatives were operating across Europe, and in Japan, Canada, and the United States. In 1997, seventeen of the labeling initiatives in Europe joined together to create the Fairtrade Labelling Organizations International (FLO) as a global umbrella organization for certification of fair trade products (Nicholls and Opal 2005). The first US-based labeling organization, Transfair USA, was formed in 1998 and situated itself under the umbrella of FLO (Conroy 2007). FLO now sets international standards for labeling of fourteen product categories and has expanded beyond food to cotton and sports balls (FLO, *Products* 2009).

A current fourth wave of fair trade that began in the 2000s is often referenced with the term "mainstreaming." Sales of fair trade agricultural commodities increasingly involved large corporations as a means of expanding the market for fair trade products (Nicholls and Opal 2005). In efforts to increase its impacts and demand of products for its expanding producer base, FLO pursued mainstreaming of fair trade commodities in conventional retailers such as Starbucks, Safeway, and Walmart in the United States (Conroy 2007). Retailers became corporate licensees for fair trade products (Fridell 2009).

Mainstreaming has been an effective tool for growth. From 2004 to 2007, retail sales of FLO certified fair trade products (primarily food commodities such as coffee, tea, cocoa, sugar, and wine) nearly tripled from $607 million to $1.74 billion. The United States accounts for 31 percent of fair trade sales, followed by the United Kingdom at 30 percent. When noncertified sales (primarily handicrafts) are added, global fair trade sales in 2007 came to $1.93 billion (Krier 2007). However, as Krier (2007) notes,

> Fair Trade—as opposed to traditional business—is not only about business success as reflected in sales figures. It is foremost about people and more particularly the ability of disadvantaged producers and workers in the Global South to improve their livelihoods and to make development work to the benefit of their families and communities. (9)

Assessment of Fair Trade Artisan Enterprise—Why Now?

Global commerce contributes to a confluence of issues. Public calls for corporate social responsibility (CSR) are evolving into demands for business accountability. Consumer attention to ethical business practices is on the ascent. Fair trade leaders ponder whether fair trade has become a marketing tool focused solely on fair wages rather than a commitment to core business standards and development practices that encompass far more than worker compensation. Development planners question the advisability of support for artisan employment as a strategy for economic and social change. The paucity of in-depth, empirical data on the linkage between artisan work and development reinforces this uncertainty (Liebl and Roy 2003). Together, concerns from a variety of quarters point to the need for assessment of socioeconomic impacts of artisan work, particularly in the handicrafts and apparel sectors, as new systems for fair trade business accountability are explored.

Within the apparel industry, these concerns are particularly salient. After a decade, when apparel businesses developed codes of conduct for labor standards and working conditions, and systems to monitor factories for compliance with these codes, limited success has been achieved (Dickson, Loker, and Eckman 2009). Some apparel businesses have begun to claim they are following fair trade practices with at least a portion of their suppliers. Exploration of the value of a development-focused fair trade approach to business is timely for both its impact for artisan enterprise as well as its applicability for global multinational apparel firms.

Industry analysts assess that as US and European corporations have given greater attention to their social and environmental practices, some have moved toward external audits and monitoring that creates public accountability for their actions (Conroy 2007; Dickson, Loker, and Eckman 2009; Porter and Kramer 2006). In a 2005 *Financial Times* article, Tobias Buck reports that one-half of the world's largest companies now share information about their environmental and social performance. Yet, many apparel businesses remain silent about their efforts in social responsibility. An analysis of websites of the 119 largest apparel brands and retailers in the United States found that only 28 percent published a code of conduct detailing expectations they had for their suppliers' labor standards and working conditions. Even fewer provided information about how the codes were implemented or findings of factory audits (Dickson and Kovaleski 2007).

Social responsibility is now evolving into calls for social accountability of a firm's business commitments. Conroy (2007) describes this transformation as "CSR with teeth" (33). After all, having a code of conduct reflects that a company is aware of some of its responsibilities; however, its presence does not indicate whether the code has been implemented. Clarkson (1995) stresses the importance of presenting performance data that reflect

> what the company is actually doing or has done with reference to specific issues.... If data about an issue are not available, that fact

in itself is important in evaluating a company's strategy or posture. When no data are available, that issue is not being managed. . . . Performance data are available whenever a particular stakeholder issue is considered by a company to be of sufficient importance to justify being managed. (108)

The transformation from social responsibility to business accountability acknowledges the needs of consumers and other stakeholders. As Ed Williams, head of Corporate Social Responsibility for the British retail leader Marks and Spencer, assesses, "The world has been moving from a 'trust me' to a 'show me' to a 'prove to me' world—and increasingly we are entering an 'involve me' world in which all our stakeholders expect to be heard and their view taken into account" (quoted in Conroy 2007, 35).

As Williams suggests, ethnical business practices of manufacturers and retailers are becoming a significant driver in consumer decision making (Shaw and Shiu 2002; Tallontire, Rentsendorj, and Blowfield 2001). In a national multiyear study among 1,000 consumers, the men and women participants resoundingly indicted that corporate support of social issues are important in building trust (Cone 2006). Nearly 86 percent of those surveyed in the 2004 Cone Corporate Citizenship study replied that they are willing to switch brands or retailers to companies that support important social causes (Cone 2006). This percentage has increased more than 30 percent since 1993. Not only do customers favor corporate support of social issues, but 86 percent of the respondents also want companies to talk more about their efforts and to place these comments center stage in business marketing and promotional campaigns. Only four in ten consumers assessed that companies were effectively telling their social responsibility story. There remain questions, however, whether the information available to apparel consumers about the conditions under which apparel is produced is adequate to support their increasing interests in social responsibility (Dickson 2005).

As another indicator of the growing salience of ethical business practices, in 1993, only 26 percent of consumers could name a company that stood out in their mind as a responsible corporate citizen. The figure rose to 80 percent in 2004. Consumers appear to be paying more attention to corporate social responsibility and to which companies commit to it. Consumers who are eighteen to twenty-five years old appear particularly vigilant as compared to other age groups. However, consumers in all age groups expect businesses to "walk the talk" through company-wide practices. Supporting social causes is not enough if the company is not also attending to the quality of their products and services, human rights in manufacturing, fair pricing, employee benefits, and laws and regulations (Cone 2006).

As specifically related to fair trade, consumers hold firm expectations for fair trade business practices (Nicholls and Opal 2005). When asked to define fair trade, over 50 percent of Canadian and US fair trade customers equated fair trade with providing a fair or living wage to artisans or farmers (Littrell, Ma, and Halepete 2005). A living wage entailed the producers earning enough to provide for their food, housing, healthcare, and education. Across generational cohorts, fair trade customers agree on their motivations for purchasing fair trade products. Consumers' consumption of fair trade products is driven by whether workers are treated with respect; products are produced in a safe, clean environment; and purchases are helping to alleviate poverty (Littrell, Ma, and Halepete 2005).

Fair trade customers differentiate between fair trade and mainstream businesses by focusing on the organizations' motivations for conducting business (Hira and Ferrie 2006; Littrell, Ma, and Halepete 2005). Attention to "people versus profits" or "builds lives, not wallets" succinctly describes customers' perceptions of the two business approaches. Whether MarketPlace is accountable to fair trade claims for improving quality of life and empowering artisans is a focus of this book.

Fair Trade in the Context of Social Responsibility and Accountability

As fair trade leaders look to the future, they question the appropriateness of large corporations adopting fair trade practices as part of their corporate social responsibility programs, as compared with fair trade embraced by smaller, "100 percent fair trade" organizations that originated the movement and practice it throughout their work. They also consider the value of an organizational certification being put in place by the WFTO (*SFTMS* 2009) as compared with a possible fair trade apparel certification. At the end of 2009, Transfair USA released for public comment a pilot factory standard for apparel and home goods that would be used to certify these products as meeting fair trade criteria (Transfair USA, *Apparel Products*). Earlier input that Transfair USA received from labor organizations demanded that standards for fair trade apparel certification would need to align with internationally recognized standards for human and worker rights and be more rigorous than those found in the codes of conduct and monitoring systems already being implemented by large corporate brands and retailers in the global apparel industry (Maquila Solidarity Network 2006).

As discussion mounts on certification, questions emerge. Would these standards be too far removed from the realities of smaller artisan groups such as those working with MarketPlace? Will increased focus on expanding the fair trade market shrink fair trade accountability for providing social benefits to small producers (Mukherjee and Reed 2009)? Will fair trade be reduced to a single issue of fair price, termed "fair trade lite," rather than the broader spectrum of business practices and values long embedded with fair trade (Gogoi 2008)? These, and other issues, form the forthcoming agenda for the WFTO as they revisit the standards and markers that serve as criteria for association membership and help consumers make judgments about fair trade.

Paul Myers, President of the WFTO, remains committed to small-scale, marginalized producer groups. Yet, he and other fair trade observers acknowledge that very little is measured in terms of social impacts and empowerment among these workers who, as members of small enterprises, are assured of long-term business commitments, fair wages, and a variety of training and educational opportunities (Layton 2004; Paul Myers, personal communication June 26, 2008). In "Fair Trade Artisan Enterprise," we assess economic and social impacts from fair trade work in a small artisan enterprise. In ensuing chapters, we describe in detail impacts that support application of a broad range of fair trade practices beyond wages as emphasized in "fair trade lite," and contemplate essential components for the practice of fair trade in both small artisan groups and large multinational corporations.

Artisans and Development

In this book, we focus on issues and challenges for the artisan sector of fair trade.[5] Within this sector, artisans produce a range of handcrafted products, including apparel, accessories, jewelry, functional and decorative household products, games and toys, paper products, and holiday items. Fair trade products are noted for their ethnic identity. Goods embody aesthetic features and production technologies enmeshed in artisans' local traditions. Some level of hand production is common; however, artisans frequently accelerate production through electrically powered machines for processing raw materials, forming products, and finishing artisanal wares.

Debate surrounds the question of whether artisan enterprises are a viable strategy for economic development (Chatterjee 2007; Joshi 2001; Liebl and Roy 2001, 2004; Morris 1996; Roy 2001). Those opposed to artisan work cite low remuneration, long hours, and intensive training as inferior to other income alternatives (Dhamija 1989; Liebl and Roy 2001). Craft production is viewed as an unpredictable, stopgap approach to development. Chatterjee, a leader in craft development in India, notes that those in power positions in India consider craft sector employment as a "fringe, feel-good activity unrelated to power and economic vitality" in the global marketplace (2007, 12). Indian government officials are prone to align handicraft work for "housewives to be done in their free time that gives them a little extra money to supplement the main income from men" (Wilkinson-Weber 1999, 87).

On the positive side, proponents argue that artisan work can realize income generation while also achieving broader social and cultural goals (Basu 1995; Bhatt 2006; Grimes and Milgram 2000; Liebl and Roy 2003, 2004; Paige-Reeves 1998; Rosenbaum and Goldin 1997; Stephen 1991; Tice 1995; Turner 2007). A growing number of international observers point to artisan enterprises as cultural industries providing a sustainable answer to employment among the poor, and contributing to artistic preservation (Liebl 2005). Employment in small entrepreneurial enterprises is viewed as increasing mobility, enhancing self-worth, and improving interpersonal skills for working across class, caste, and ethnic boundaries in India (MacHenry 2000). As Rosenbaum (2000), a longtime activist with women's artisan groups, stated, "the productive and transformative potential of women working together for the welfare of their families and communities is immense" (105). However, Wilkinson-Weber (1999) warns not to assume that a women-only artisan endeavor leads to equity in production or lack of internal conflict.

While a handful of scholars enlighten the debate through their empirical investigations, all too often the contentious discussion is fueled by philosophical positioning and anecdotal evidence. Walter Morris (1996), a longtime participant in craft development, offered a pragmatic challenge to the discourse. "Artisans are not going to disappear in the new millennium and neither will their contributions to our daily lives and culture. The time has come to rethink their position" (150).

Participation in the debate is critical for the very poor who turn to artisan production as an avenue for escaping poverty. After agriculture and tourism, artisan work provides a significant source of income in many less developed countries (Basu 1995). However, by the twenty-first century, artisans in diverse regions of the world lost local patronage upon which they depended, as cheaper, mass-produced alternatives flooded their rural villages. For many artisan enterprises, participation in regional, tourism, and export markets is essential to their survival (Littrell and Dickson 1999).

For India, the artisan debate is particularly important, given the 90 percent of Indians who work in the informal economy and the size of the artisan sector within the nation's economy (Luce 2007). In 2000, handicrafts contributed $6.1 billion in sales in India, up from $4.6 billion in 1994. Global exports accounted for between $1.9 and $4 billion, an increase from $1.3 billion. Between eight and nine million people were fully or partially employed in the sector in 2000 (Liebl and Roy 2003, 2004). India's craft tradition is well described by Joshi (2001):

> The intensive strength of the crafts sector is that it grows from a tradition of indigenous creativity and is interwoven with the fabric of society. Crafts are an integral part of the Indian lifestyle, and are strongly associated with festivals, religion, art, architecture, performing arts, sculpture and paintings, as well as many of the everyday happenings of life. (6)

At the time of independence in 1947, the Indian government enhanced its support for handicraft development by forming the All India Handicrafts Board. The board served as an umbrella for marketing venues throughout India, including the Central Cottage Industries Emporium. In the ensuing years, a variety of nongovernmental organizations (NGOs) formed to support handicrafts. Perhaps best known across India is SEWA (Self-Employed Women's Association), with programs for microcredit and for domestic and export marketing of crafts under its broad umbrella of women-led initiatives (Bhatt 2006). Other NGOs, more regional in focus, such as Kala Rashka and Kutch Mahila Vikas Sangathan in Kutch, support artisan participation in designing, pricing, and marketing of crafts as a means to expand embroidery traditions and generate income in the commercial market (Frater 2002).

By the 1990s, the Indian government shifted its focus from internal marketing to building capacity among NGOs for assisting in artisan enterprise development, providing design and technical input, and establishing alternative platforms to the earlier retail emporiums. These initiatives were intended to back the increasing focus on exports as a means of sector development. However, difficulty in accessing viable new markets remains an ongoing challenge (Liebl and Roy 2001).

In summary, concerns from business leaders, fair trade participants and scholars, and artisan development planners contribute to a climate for artisan employment that is disquieting to some while suggesting potential opportunities to others. It is timely to consider the claims made about fair trade. MarketPlace: Handwork of India offers a fair trade approach that is opportune for analysis and from which lessons may be learned that inform the fair trade movement and its developing policies related to certification, artisan enterprise employment, and broader concerns about social responsibility and accountability. Understanding artisan impacts from employment with a fair trade enterprise sheds light on whether support from the public and private sectors is warranted for artisan enterprise development. How artisan work and quality of life are linked is contemplated for its effectiveness in small enterprise development within the fair trade movement and for its potential relevance to fair trade apparel certification policy. In addition, a methodology for assessing fair trade accountability illustrates the diverse social and economic impacts resulting from a broad range of fair trade business practices. Finally, how income generation and social development can be combined provides consumers with a benchmark for assessing fair trade success within the larger framework of business accountability.

Questions for Fair Trade Analysis

A series of questions guided our exploration of fair trade for its impacts on artisans' lives and its relevance to business social responsibility and accountability. As the chapters unfold, we ask the following questions:

1. What principles and practices underlie the MarketPlace approach for integrating business and development? How does the MarketPlace approach fit the cultural context for artisans residing in the slums of Mumbai?

2. How has artisan work with MarketPlace impacted the capabilities, livelihood, and well-being of women textile artisans in India? How does the MarketPlace approach inform broader understanding on quality of life?

3. What do workers like those with MarketPlace stand to gain or lose from fair trade apparel certification? What recommendations can be made to fair trade apparel certifying organizations based on the MarketPlace experience?

4. What can 100% Fair Trade organizations like MarketPlace learn from the global apparel industry's decade-long effort to address worker and human rights?

5. What insights are gained for support of artisan enterprise development? Is artisan work a survival or asset-building strategy? Does MarketPlace provide "decent work" that allows artisans voice and recognition, stability, personal development, fairness, and equality?

Our answers to these questions are grounded in the data from our interviews and interactions with MarketPlace artisans. They are also framed within broader theoretical and applied discussions that address grassroots development theory, business social responsibility and accountability and the fair trade movement, and challenges faced by craft enterprises in the global marketplace.

Methods for Conducting the Analysis

In conducting our socioeconomic audit, we employed a variety of techniques to carry out field research in India across an eight-year period beginning in the late 1990s. In our multimethod approach, we participated in design and product development sessions; met with artisans in their workshops; observed all aspects of fabric and garment production, quality inspection, and shipping; visited with artisans' in their homes; and took part in social activities. Formal interviewing with 161 artisans occurred between 2001 and 2003. During two follow-up trips in 2004 and 2007, group leaders were interviewed about their groups' growth and change.

The Earthwatch Institute funded the formal interviewing portion of our research. A criterion of the funder is that citizen volunteers be integral to the research. Over three years, twenty-three volunteer research assistants from Australia, Canada, England, and the United States joined us in two-week intervals for conducting interviews. Upon arrival in Mumbai, the volunteers received two and one-half days of training to familiarize them with Market-Place, SHARE, the artisan workshops, and the Golibar slum, including visits with artisans in their homes. The interview topics and interviewing techniques were introduced and practiced. Greater detail describing the research approach and data analysis is provided in the book's appendix.

Our work is also informed by our longtime engagement with theories and practices of fair trade organizations and their directors other than MarketPlace, and with leaders in multinational business social responsibility and accountability. Across the past twenty years, Mary Littrell has focused on artisan enterprises, with particular emphasis on how textile artisan enterprises achieve sustainability in the increasingly competitive market for artisan products. In the early 2000s, she was part of a Ford Foundation funded team that assessed impacts and sustainability issues for Aid to Artisan supported artisan projects in Armenia, Ghana, and Central Asian countries of Uzbekistan, the Kyrgyz Republic, and Kazakhstan. While living in Malaysia with her family, she worked with the Malaysian Handicraft Development Corporation on textile product development for the international tourist market. Marsha Dickson's membership on the board of directors of the Fair Labor Association uniquely positioned her to participate in and observe the work that was being carried out by the multistakeholder initiative and the apparel brands and retailers leading efforts in corporate social responsibility. Additional research focused on social responsibility in the mainstream apparel industry has included interviews with industry and NGO professionals, interactions with industry associations, reading of hundreds of reports on the issues, and visits to numerous apparel factories around the world.

We have divided the book into three sections for addressing our guiding questions. Section I establishes the background and rational for the book. In this first chapter, we have introduced MarketPlace: Handwork of India and the underlying topics of fair trade, business social responsibility and accountability, and artisan enterprise. Chapter 2 describes the scholarly frameworks and contemporary debates that served as context for our arguments. Chapter 3 offers an in-depth description of MarketPlace's evolution as a business and development organization.

In Section II, we examine social and economic impacts in the form of capabilities, livelihood, and well-being. Chapter 4 provides a photodocumented context of artisans' typical days, assesses the need for flexibility and nonlinearity of work, and introduces the artisans, their families, and their employment history prior to joining MarketPlace. In Chapter 5, a range of acquired skills offers evidence of new capabilities for communication, business planning, interpersonal support, problem solving, and entrepreneurship. Artisan's income and expenditures are examined in detail in Chapter 6. The question of whether artisans are acquiring a living wage is raised in this chapter. Finally, in Chapter 7 we discuss forms of material, psychological, and social well-being ranging across improved housing, psychological refuge found within production units, and household decision making.

Section III provides conclusions from our analysis. Chapter 8 returns to the five sets of questions guiding our research about artisan enterprise and impacts from fair trade. Our conclusions illuminate successes and ongoing challenges for conducting business, with a dual focus on generating income in the profit-driven global marketplace and on developing capabilities for the empowerment of low-income artisans. We connect our findings to the concerns raised by business leaders, fair trade directors, labor activists, and artisan development planners. Discussion about artisan enterprise centers on social responsibility and accountability as evidenced by artisan capabilities, livelihood and quality of life, work–household interface, living wages, and fair trade certification. We also contemplate the insights that fair trade organizations can gain from the broader apparel industry's efforts to address worker rights. Finally, we reflect on the MarketPlace fair trade model as a survival or asset-building strategy and as a paradigm for providing decent work.

Notes

1. Throughout our interviews at MarketPlace, we assured the artisans of anonymity in any of our writing that resulted from the research. Accordingly, pseudonyms have been used throughout the text to protect artisans' identities.

2. Ownership of a 10-by-10-ft home is a goal of Mumbai slum residents. The term derives from the standard length of building and roofing materials used for housing construction in the slums.

3. SHARE was founded by Pushpika Freitas's mother, a noted social worker in India, with special attention given to men and women suffering from leprosy. Today, SHARE's focus has expanded more broadly to social and economic development of the poor.

4. For a more extensive discussion of fair trade origins and overviews of major US fair trade organizations, see Littrell, M. A., and Dickson, M. A. 1999. *Social responsibility in the global market: Fair trade of cultural products.* Thousand Oaks, CA: Sage.

5. Other scholars address the agricultural sector of fair trade, giving attention to the position of fair trade agriculture in world commodity markets. These commodities include coffee, tea, spices, chocolate, fruit, fish, and flowers. For an overview of issues and challenges in the agriculture sector of fair trade, see Murray, D. L., Raynolds, L. T., and Taylor, P. L. 2003. *Poverty alleviation and fair trade coffee in Latin America.* Fort Collins, CO: Colorado State University Fair Trade Research Group; Raynolds, L. T., Murray, D. L., and Wilkinson, J. (Eds.) 2007. *Fair trade: The challenges of transforming globalization.* London: Routledge.

CHAPTER 2

Perspectives for Evaluating Artisan Enterprise

Our case study of MarketPlace: Handwork of India (MarketPlace) illuminates the everyday experiences of a group of artisans laboring to earn a living within the larger framework of global commerce. More specifically, we focus on the particularity of the fair trade experience (Guyer, Denzer, and Agbaje 2002). E. P. Thompson (1978) espouses the value of assessing daily life for insights into broader concerns and new ways of thinking.

> Experience walks in without knocking at the door, and announces deaths, crises of subsistence, trench warfare, unemployment, inflation, genocide. People starve; their survivors think in new ways about the market. People are imprisoned; in prison they meditate in new ways about the law. In the face of such general experiences old conceptual systems may crumble and new problematics insist upon their presence. (11)

As scholars, we are warned, however, that "description alone of 'the way things are' will not do. One also needs to address the momentum that experience builds up in various corners of economic life" (Guyer, Denzer, and Agbaje 2002, x). Michel de Certeau (1984) further challenges that considerations of everyday "'ways of operating,' or doing things no longer appear as merely the obscure background of social activity" (xi), but that in penetrating these "ways of operating" we might encounter perspectives for addressing our questions raised in Chapter 1 related to artisan enterprise, fair trade, and social responsibility.

A snapshot of Indian socioeconomic conditions in 2010 provides context to our analysis of life at MarketPlace. With a population of over 1.3 billion, India is the world's largest democracy with a "booming but peculiarly lopsided economy" (Luce 2007, 8). As India leaps into global economic prominence with a GDP (Purchasing Power Parity) that is fifth in the world, it also serves as home to a population with an average annual income below $1,000 (*2009 CIA World Fact Book*; Luce 2007). India ranks 134 out of 182 countries on the United Nations Human Development Index (HDI), a measure that integrates life expectancy, literacy and school enrollment, and standard of living statistics (*Human Development Report* 2009). For women, using the gender-related development index (GDI), 89% of the 155 countries where a GDI has been figured have a higher GDI than India. (*Human Development Report* 2009).

Less than 10 percent of India's labor force is employed in the formal economy; 4 percent of India's working women have formal sector positions (Hill 2001). Labeled by India as the "organized sector," nearly two-thirds work as employees of the government with some measure of accompanying job security. The much-heralded IT (information technology) sector offers employment to only one-quarter of 1 percent of the population and, while boosting India's self-confidence and global importance, is not judged to be "an answer to the hopes of the majority of India's job-hungry masses" (Luce 2007, 48). In contrast, the remaining 90 percent, including nearly all of India's artisan sector, make up the "unorganized economy." Artisans are joined by Indians who are

> milking the family cow; making up the seasonal armies of mobile casual farmworkers; running small shops or street side stalls; making incense sticks and bidis; driving rickshaws, working as maids, gardeners, and night watchmen; and bashing metal as mechanics in small-town repair shops. (Luce 2007, 47)

These individuals toil without protection in the form of employment contracts, union or legislative protection, and social benefits often available to those in formal sector positions (Hill 2001).

Scholars, development planners, fair trade and labor activists, and artisan enterprise leaders provide a range of perspectives that informed our analysis of MarketPlace. In an initial section, models are introduced for assessing quality of life and human development. The second section focuses on fair trade, including perspectives on emerging certification strategies. The urgent topic of living wages and their measurement is discussed in this section as well. In a third section, the artisan sector in India is explored for current challenges and encouraging initiatives for enterprise sustainability.

Quality of Life and Human Development

Researchers acknowledge that quality of life is complex and multi-dimensional. Understanding quality of life includes acknowledging people's assets and vulnerabilities, their strategies for exploiting and expanding their assets, and their access or barriers to resources (Turner 2007). Of particular relevance to this book is the relationship between work and quality of life for MarketPlace artisans and their families. Ela Bhatt (2008), founder of SEWA (Self Employed Women's Association)—India's NGO of poor, informal sector women workers, emphasized in a speech to the heads of state gathered at the United Nations,

> A word that is largely absent from the [UN] Development goals is work. In my experience, the link between poverty and growth is decent work. Decent work means full employment at the household level; it builds the local economy and strengthens a community. Employers are constantly searching the globe for cheap labor; but the jobs they create abroad cannot build a society or even a sustainable economy.

Within India, researchers have linked quality of life with work using a variety of indicators. In Northern Indian villages, Basic Minimum Needs (BMNs) for families included food, health, hospital services, employment, drinking water, and relief from a heavy workload (Brinkerhoff, Fredell, and Frideres 1997). Of these, employment satisfaction was closely related to quality of life, indicating a spillover effect where work satisfaction permeates many areas of life. For women, work satisfaction was especially pivotal in overall assessment of life quality. In another approach to exploring quality of life, Indian respondents were asked to describe goals for their lives. Among poor city dwellers, Indian respondents focused on family improvements as life goals. Enhancing their children's well-being was viewed as a direct contribution from life at work (Mukherjee 1981).

Life satisfaction has also been closely connected with strong social relationships, another theme for our analysis of MarketPlace artisans (Biswas-Diener and Diener 2001). While slum dwellers in Kolkata experienced a lower sense of life satisfaction than more affluent comparison groups, their overall satisfaction was not as low as expected for a city closely associated with Indian poverty. Slum dwellers, while poor, lived in well-established communities as compared to the sex workers and pavement dwellers who formed other populations in the study. In addition, nonmaterial resources such as strong social relationships emerged as important in understanding slum dwellers' well-being. The researchers concluded that "to the extent the poor can utilize their strong social relationships, the negative effects of poverty are counterbalanced" (347).

Social science scholars from a broad range of disciplines provide models for examining quality of life and human development. Four of these perspectives proved useful in exploring the experiences of Marketplace artisans. These include a five-part model of capabilities, livelihood, and well-being proposed by Robert Chambers, an international development scholar. Amartya Sen and Martha Nussbaum, economist and philosopher, respectively, enlarge on capabilities and their enactment. Elizabeth Hill, a political economist, argues for the concept of agency as a precursor of capabilities. Finally, Femida Handy (public policy and environmental studies), Meenaz Kassam (education), Suzanne Feeney (nonprofit management), and Bhagyashree Ranade (marketing) provide insights from their analysis of Indian NGOs, a common organizational structure in the artisan sector. Their model of high-impact NGOs reinforces and further integrates a variety of variables introduced by the previous scholars.

Model of Well-Being

As Robert Chambers looked into the twenty-first century, he assessed, "More people than ever before are wealthy beyond any reasonable need for a good life, and more are poor and vulnerable below any conceivable definition of decency" (1997, 1). In addressing this inequity, he succinctly summarized the emergent paradigm shift in development policy of

> Putting people first. . . . A massive shift in priorities and thinking has been taking place, from things and infrastructure to people and capabilities. Consonant with this shift, five words, taken together, seem to capture and express much of an emerging consensus. These are well-being, livelihood, capability, equity and sustainability. (Chambers 1997, 9)

In our analysis, we subscribe to Chambers' five-part model as a framework for assessing impacts of fair trade artisan enterprises. In Chambers' model, well-being differs from wealth or poverty by encompassing a range of social, psychological, and spiritual indicators. Livelihood undergirds well-being and flows from a dependable source of cash and food to meet basic needs. Capabilities, conceptualized by Chambers as the bedrock and starting point for development, contribute to livelihood and well-being. Capabilities are acquired and enlarged through learning, training, and practice. If choices must be made, Chambers' model favors equity among the poor by "putting the last first" (11). Finally, conditions that foster long-term sustainability of livelihood and well-being form the core of development policy.

Capabilities and Enactment

Sen and Nussbaum concentrate on people's capabilities as central to development. For Sen (1980), the utility of a capabilities approach is for comparative discussions of quality of life in terms of what people are able to do. Nussbaum (2000) describes their emphasis on capabilities: "instead of asking about people's satisfactions, or how much in the way of resources they are able to command, we ask, instead, about what they are actually able to do or be" (12).

Sen distinguishes between acquiring human capabilities and using those capabilities. Capabilities, as a resource, have little value without their application. Hill (2001) succinctly summarizes this position as applied to development.

> The capabilities approach required that policy makers move from asking, "What does a worker need to be more productive?" to "What is a worker actually able to do or be?" Providing marginalized workers with access to productive resources such as credit, vocational training or technology will only produce the intended change if the person is able to both access the resource and implement their newfound skills. (445)

Sen (1980, 1993) goes on to distinguish that people also require the social and personal freedom to choose to access resources that may contribute to their well-being. Well-being freedom describes the freedom to access resources that develop capabilities and well-being achievement alludes to the freedom to choose how to use or apply capabilities and improve well-being. Central to Sen's arguments is the requisite that people have the freedom to both acquire and apply capabilities, an assumption that may be constrained by social norms and religious practices, as is the case among Indian women living in poverty (Handy, Kassam, Feeney, and Ranade 2006).

Nussbaum (2000) contributes to the discussion on capabilities by proposing a list of what she considers to be central, interconnected human functional components (see Table 2.1). Nussbaum asserts that the capabilities approach not only provides an orientation for measuring quality of life but also "can serve as the foundation for constitutional guarantees to which nations should be held by their citizens" (2000, 298). She summarizes their importance for women.

> Women in much of the world lose out by being women. Their human powers of choice and sociability are frequently thwarted by societies in which they must live as the adjuncts and servants of the ends of others and in which their sociability is deformed by fear and hierarchy. But they are bearers of human capabilities, basic powers of choice that make a moral claim for opportunities to be realized and flourish. Women's unequal failure to attain a higher level of capability, at which the choice of central human functions is really open to them, is therefore a problem of justice (298).

Table 2.1 Central human functional capabilities[a]

CAPABILITY	DESCRIPTION (ADAPTED)
Life	Able to live to the end of a human life of normal length
Bodily health	Being able to have good health, including reproductive health, and adequate nutrition and shelter
Bodily integrity	Being able to move freely from place to place with one's bodily boundaries treated as sovereign, having opportunity for sexual satisfaction and choice in reproduction
Senses, imagination, and thought	Being able to use the senses to imagine, think, and reason, informed by an adequate education
Emotions	Being able to have attachments to things and people, without overwhelming fear or anxiety, or by traumatic abuse or neglect
Practical reason	Being able to form a conception of the good and to engage in critical reflection about the planning of one's life
Affiliation	Being able to live with and toward others, including showing concern for others, engaging in social interaction; being treated as a dignified being with worth equal to others
Other species	Being able to live with concern for animals, plants, and the world of nature
Play	Being able to laugh, play, and enjoy recreational activities
Control over one's environment	Being able to participate in political choices that govern one's life; having property rights; having the right to seek employment on an equal basis with others

[a]Nussbaum (2000, 78-80).

Agency as a Precursor of Capabilities

Hill (2001) suggests that before capabilities can be acquired and applied, there must be agency, or an ability to act that is predicated on self- and interpersonal respect, and recognition gained through solidarity and collective action. Hill's assessment is grounded in an in-depth, qualitative study of Indian informal sector women associated with SEWA, the largest trade union and NGO of informal sector workers, of which a significant number are involved in artisan work. Hill bases her analysis on Axel Honneth's *The Struggle for Recognition* (1995), in which he asserts that moral injury and non-recognition are significant experiences that undermine human agency and

Table 2.2 SEWA pathway to identity formation and economic development

Stages in progression	→ Collective organizing. Interpersonal recognition.	→ Self-realization. Worker identity.	→ Ability to act. Agency.	→ Increased productivity. Economic development and work life reform.

Note: Adapted from Hill (2001).

that self-respect, self-confidence, and interpersonal recognition are essential for the activation of agency. Through her analysis of SEWA members and their collective activities, Hill provides a series of stages through which SEWA women progress in identity formation (see Table 2.2). Interaction and collective involvement with other workers at SEWA was essential to this progression. Interpersonal and mutual recognition emerged as the SEWA women took part in joint activities that involved training and discussion of common problems and solutions for daily life, employment, and group advancement. These joint activities promoted self-identity and confidence that then led to agency for acquisition of skills and capabilities. As these capabilities were acquired and applied, they carried over into activation of strategies for negotiating and strengthening social and cultural position and to contributions within the family and among community members.

High-Impact NGOs

Finally, Handy et al. (2006) draw from their research with twenty Indian NGOs to propose a model of high-impact, female NGOs. The researchers assess that high impact is reached when an NGO is

> raising women's awareness in a holistic way, so that they are not only educated, healthy, or able to run a micro-financed enterprise, but that she can eventually effectively navigate the way in the socio-cultural environment in which she functions. Such empowerment . . . depends largely on the development of the capacity to exercise a certain amount of control over the social, economic, and political conditions that determine her life. (130)

Several parts of their model demonstrated usefulness for application in our analysis. These include the importance of female leadership in a solely or largely female NGO, vertical integration, and generational activities. The female NGO leaders, all classified as feminists, passionately promoted social justice through collective, inclusive, and consensus-building approaches to NGO development. A supportive family, family role models, higher education, and experience in social services undergirded the women's tireless leadership. High vertical integration involves an NGO sequentially adding programs and services to complement the original core activity and, through multiplier effects, promoting holistic development. Examples could include programs centered on reproductive health, youth tutoring, and family counseling. Generational activities, as seminally described by Korten (1987), refer to growth in how an NGO helps its members. First generational activities provide for basic human needs, whereas over time the organization progresses into higher generational activities that foster capacity building, advocacy, decision making, and inter-NGO networking for promoting a broader social vision of human development.

Each of these models fed into our analysis in unique ways. Across the work of these eminent scholars, we gained perspectives on three-part conceptualization of capabilities, livelihood, and well-being; differentiation between capability acquisition and application; operationalization of agency and capability acquisition, and organizational characteristics that promote holistic development of members. Together, this overview of quality of life and development studies in India and elsewhere pointed to the critical need to assess a broad range of indicators in documenting outcomes from artisan employment in fair trade. Gathering both quantitative and qualitative data was essential for understanding how artisans conceptualize impacts, stability, and change in their lives and for comparison of our research to that of previous scholars.

Fair Trade

In Chapter 1, we introduced the concept of fair trade and the post–World War II emergence of US-based fair trade businesses that sold primarily handicrafts and were referred to as alternative trading organizations (ATOs). Through the ensuing decades, alternative or fair trade businesses would evolve and grow, shifting from mission-focused organizations that were trying to engage in business to "businesses with a mission." This redirection came about as the marketplace became saturated with ethnic-inspired, imported products, making it necessary for ATOs to begin working on product development in collaboration with artisans rather than simply buying whatever artisans had to offer for stocking their fair trade stores (Paul Leatherman, personal communication June 23, 2008). Even with these changes, organizations originating the fair trade movement and working in the handicraft sector continued working toward a long-term goal of creating a compatible, nonexploitive, and humanizing system of international exchange. They also advocated transparency of business practices among trading partners (European Fair Trade Association 2008).

Despite the "100% Fair Trade" goals and commitments of organizations like Ten Thousand Villages and MarketPlace, the fair trade movement began to diverge as a result of creation of certification programs, a primary focus on agricultural commodities, and expanded involvement of corporations. The emergence of fair trade certification required establishing clear standards that would be met, a process of verifying compliance to the standards, and a label that would mark fair trade products and offer accountability to the broader public (Conroy 2007). As the Fairtrade Labelling Organizations (FLO) and the various national labeling initiatives established fair trade standards for agricultural products, an increasing emphasis was placed on simple to measure economic criteria, such as extra income received as a result of fair trade sales. Projects to expand capabilities and make holistic impacts on development and quality of life through relationships that had been built at the grassroots level and had been commitments of ATOs seemed to be traded off for a more singular focus on economic growth, an expanded market, and the greater visibility that corporations could bring (Mukherjee and Reed 2009; Nicholls and Opal 2005; Renard 2005). Reed (2009) explains the significance of this change as follows.

> While corporate participation has the potential to rapidly extend the market for fair trade goods, it threatens key aspects of what many see as the original vision of fair trade—most notably a primary concern for the plight of small producers and the goal of developing an alternative approach to trade and development—and may even be undermining [fair trade's] long-term survival. (3)

As corporate retailers began to be involved in sale of fair trade products, FLO selectively allowed use of plantation farms in order to open some agricultural markets that had no small producers. But the practice was later extended to other markets where there *were* small producers and in some cases larger plantations replaced the smaller farms (Fridell 2007; Keahey, Littrell, and Murray forthcoming). Separate standards meeting the needs of large volume producers were created, but some fair trade producers continued following fair trade principles without seeking certification (Nicholls and Opal 2005; Reed 2009).

Fair Trade Apparel Certification

In 2004, FLO created standards and processes for certifying fair trade cotton. Small farmers were required to be organized into cooperatives or other democratic groups that are paid fair trade minimum prices and premiums above the cost of goods that are used by the cooperatives in any way they choose (Quigley and Opal 2006). While the certification covered only the growing of cotton, it was expected by FLO that the ginning through garment finishing stages would demonstrate efforts to comply with key International Labour Organization (ILO) conventions detailing labor standards for hours of work, forced labor, freedom of association, and others. The fair trade cotton certification program, however, had no way of monitoring and verifying the conditions under which end products were actually manufactured. As a result, some consumers and organizations were confused about what the certification covered (Nicholls and Opal 2005).

Adding to the confusion was the troubled situation the mainstream apparel industry was facing in the mid-1990s, as evidence emerged that workers producing name-brand apparel and footwear in factories around the world and in the United States were paid far below legal minimum wages and forced to work long hours under conditions that were unsafe and unhealthy (see Dickson, Loker, and Eckman 2009). Over the next decade, much work would take place in the global apparel industry in efforts to improve labor standards and working conditions for factory employees around the world. Several multistakeholder initiatives were formed, including the US-based Fair Labor Association (FLA) and Social Accountability International (SAI) that work in partnership with large brands and retailers, labor organizations and trade unions, and NGOs to develop codes of conduct for factory production and processes for monitoring compliance to the codes. While the systems have failed to provide solutions for all problems industrial workers face, the multistakeholder initiatives are the best systems currently available for empowering garment workers and improving their working conditions (Dickson, Loker, and Eckman 2009; Quigley and Opal 2006).

Corporate brands and retailers have been referred to as recognizing "ethical trade," labor rights, or corporate social responsibility (CSR). For many apparel businesses, CSR has been carried out as a defensive response to major problems that have erupted in their vast global garment supply chains (Dickson, Loker, and Eckman 2009) and thus is very different than fair trade as originally practiced with small producers. Yet, new brands such as Fair Indigo are claiming to practice fair trade in their factory production of apparel (see www.fairindigo.com). Furthermore, Smith and Barrientos (2005) note that other similarities are emerging, especially as apparel brands shift their focus to capacity building and longer-term partnerships with suppliers. Standards that prioritize fair or living wages and freedom of association are also of increasing priority in CSR as they have been with FLO's certification programs (see Dickson, Loker, and Eckman 2009). Also, with fair trade products now being sourced from large plantation farms, a parallel situation would exist if apparel brands could source fair trade garments from large factories (Smith and Barrientos 2005).

In 2006, Transfair USA studied the feasibility of fair trade apparel certification by surveying and interviewing representatives of labor rights organizations and unions, fair trade organizations and ATOs, producers, academics, and various-sized brands and retail companies. Their in-depth report outlined the complexities of the global apparel supply chain and included stakeholder support and concerns if fair trade apparel certification was to be developed (Quigley and Opal 2006). By late 2009, the organization had issued a draft standard for fair trade apparel and home products, including obligations of factories and of buyers. Just as certification of agricultural commodities and participation of corporate retailers and large-scale plantation farms had stirred controversy within the fair trade movement, some of the same concerns carried over to fair trade apparel certification, including whether to focus on small or large producers or involve corporations, what standards to apply, and how to empower workers.

Whether to Involve Only Small or Large Producers and Corporations?

Fair trade experts interviewed in the Transfair USA study believed that certification should be limited to small producers (Quigley and Opal 2006). The Maquila Solidarity Network (MSN 2006) and other labor rights organizations were initially against fair trade for corporations because some retailers seemed to be trying to sell a small portion of fair trade product to improve their reputation, without maintaining credible and transparent CSR programs. Labor organizations demanded that if corporations were to be involved with fair trade garment certification, the standards for certification would have to be as strong if not stronger than the existing codes of conducts and monitoring systems used within the apparel industry (MSN 2006). Transfair USA ultimately concluded that the standard needed to be universal, but that it should take a progressive approach that would meet the needs of small and large businesses. But in their 2006 report, the organization revealed how difficult this would be, explaining,

> One brand we spoke with sources garments sewn in large, state-of-the art facilities, certified by several third parties against many different brand codes of conduct. Another imports garments made "by women who have set up their sewing machines in an overturned shipping container." (Quigley and Opal 2006, 54)

Transfair USA claims that the 2009 *Pilot Program for Fair Trade Certified Apparel & Home Goods* "is not meant to apply strictly to factories with hired labor; cooperative organizations are encouraged to participate as well" (2). Yet the standards are titled, "Obligations of CMT Facilities" and "factories" are mentioned throughout. CMT stands for "cut, make and trim," a term that has for years been used in the apparel industry in reference to factories, often offshore, that assemble garments that are designed by brand name businesses. Therefore, it seemed the standard for apparel certification was geared toward the factories producing for large corporate brands who wished to sell a small line of fair trade garments. We considered this emerging initiative in our analysis of MarketPlace and how the women working in its small workshops would be impacted, as they compete with large factories for fair trade certification.

What Standards to Apply?

In presenting initial ideas about how fair trade certification might be extended to cover apparel, Robinson and Athreya (2005) recommended that "we need a simple criterion, relatively easy to verify, which can be used as the basis for certifying the subset of all producers who will be connected up with conscientious consumers" (8). Because having a long list of labor standards is difficult and expensive to monitor and enforce, there needs to be a democratic union, with workers provided a voice in determining their wages, benefits and working conditions. Small producers could exchange the criterion of a democratic union for a certified cooperative.

In the Transfair USA study, many stakeholders indicated that a fair trade garment certification would only add value beyond the existing codes and monitoring systems, and CSR programs in the apparel industry, if it included the most rigorous standards. Particularly, it would need to be in line with the ILO's Fundamental Principles and Rights at Work, including abolition of child labor and forced labor, nondiscrimination, and freedom of association and collective bargaining, and include payment of a living wage (Quigley and Opal 2006). Yet, a fair trade expert cited in the study suggests that those involved in the 100% Fair Trade movement would be looking for standards to focus on the core development values of the fair trade movement.

> If FLO and TransFair introduce a fair trade textile standard (or any other product certification) that we feel is incongruous with the empowerment-based fair trade proposition that we have been presenting to our supporters, it would be difficult for [our organization] to continue its unqualified public support of fair trade certification. (Quigley and Opal 2006, 56)

The draft standard for Fair Trade Certified Apparel and Home Goods issued by Transfair USA lays out standards for wages and fair trade premium payments, as well as core labor standards that are based on the ILO conventions and practices by the major global multistakeholder initiatives (Transfair USA 2009). The core development goals embraced by early fair trade organizations are not evident in the standard. As we carried out our analysis of MarketPlace, we considered the likelihood that they could obtain fair trade garment certification, whether certain practices would lose relevance under this program, and how that would impact workers' lives.

How to Empower Workers?

With existing fair trade certification of agricultural commodities, social empowerment had been operationalized by requiring a committee of workers and management that has been democratically elected to identify and distribute a social premium payment for community and other development projects (Quigley and Opal 2006). In the global apparel industry's CSR movement, empowerment had been linked to attaining Fundamental Principles and Rights at Work established by the ILO's tripartite membership of business, government, and labor (Dickson, Loker, and Eckman 2009). A key element to these is the right of workers to join trade unions (MSN 2006). Mukherjee and Reed (2009) express concerns about the focus on increasing fair trade workers' ability to use industrial relations mechanisms and negotiate pay and working conditions, rather than involving them in "larger decision-making questions regarding production, investment and marketing strategies (which are the realms in which the actual decisions as to whether to participate in fair trade are made)" (6). The draft standard for fair trade apparel certification issued by Transfair USA indicates that

> Worker empowerment and development is at the core of Fair Trade certification. In our efforts in this industry, the primary focus on achieving this is through the rights of freedom of association and income that

meets workers' basic needs. The Fair Trade standard seeks to go above and beyond the norm in the industry on those and other issues consistent with the Fair Trade philosophy. (Transfair USA 2009, 2)

Cooperative ownership is allowable for producers to demonstrate that the workplace environment is "supportive of the creation of credible and functioning trade unions and/or worker committees" (6). Our analysis of the empowerment-focused activities carried out by MarketPlace was mindful of the differing perspectives on what constitutes empowerment and the fact that some MarketPlace workplaces may not meet the emerging apparel certification program's requirements for demonstrating empowerment.

Wage Standards

Wages have been a key component for FLO certification of agricultural commodities. FLO sets prices for specific agricultural commodities that reflect a minimum price that allows producers to cover costs necessary to produce the commodities in sustainable ways (FLO, *Aims of Fair Trade Standards*). The tremendous variety in apparel products does not allow a single price to be set for this product category; thus, the discussion about wages has been more focused on pursuit of either minimum or living wages, though more recently, new strategies are being explored to ensure that workers' wages are fair.

An ongoing debate about the appropriate wage floor for corporate apparel industry codes of conduct has labor activists and trade unions arguing for a living wage while many apparel brands and retailers wish to settle for a standard that simply tries to ensure their factories start paying legal minimum wages. Legal minimum wages are the lowest amount that can be paid to a worker according to local law (Dickson, Loker, and Eckman 2009). Most brands and retailers have avoided requiring a higher living wage because of difficulties in setting the appropriate wage in all their production sites, ensuring that factories actually pay the workers the appropriate wage, and the potential competitive disadvantage they might face if passing on the charges to consumers (Dickson, Loker, and Eckman 2009). In a study conducted on behalf of the FLA with factories in China and several other Asian countries, Daniel Vaughan-Whitehead (2009), senior advisor to the Wages and Working Conditions Program for the ILO, found that nearly one-quarter of the factories surveyed paid starting wages below the legal minimum. Nearly one out of five factories had trouble paying wages at all and 58 percent reported underpaying wages, especially regarding overtime. These findings give some credence to the claims of apparel brands and retailers that progress would be made if workers were paid minimum wages.

A living wage is one that supplies enough income to provide a worker and family with the basic needs and money to participate in culturally necessary activities and to set aside for a better future (Dickson, Loker, and Eckman 2009); however, there is disagreement about what basic needs should be included in the concept (Bremer 2002; Business for Social Responsibility 2002). Basic needs describe what is required for a minimum level of living for the poorest people and are considered when determining a country's poverty line (US Department of Labor 2000). The most fundamental of basic needs are food, water, housing, and safety (Okafor 1985). Additional basic needs could include transportation and education (Brinkerhoff, Fredell, and Frideres 1997).

How to calculate a living wage for apparel production remains complex because it is unique to each country and dependent on cultural and development differences in what is "necessary" and "acceptable" (Center for Reflection, Education and Action, *Sustainable living wages and income* n.d.). A 1998 Living Wage Summit identified basic needs as nutrition, clothing, healthcare, education, water, childcare, transportation, housing, and energy. The actual amounts of these basic needs can be determined by the expenditures made by families at the poverty line, or by calculating the costs of a "market basket" of goods needed for survival (US Department of Labor 2000). As a result of this summit, *living wage* was defined as the amount of money needed to cover the minimum amount of these basic needs for an average household, divided by the number of adult wage earners living in the average household, and then adding 10 percent of income for savings (Business for Social Responsibility 2002).

A recently developed Asia Floor Wage provides somewhat simpler methods for developing a minimum living wage for six countries using a market basket approach for food costs and estimating nonfood costs as equivalent to food costs. A sum for each country reflects the wages necessary to cover basic food and nonfood costs for a worker and three dependents. Exchange rates, purchasing power parity, and an averaging process are then used to identify a common wage across the six countries in hopes of preventing the countries from competing against each other by slashing worker wages and costs of production (Asia Floor Wage Alliance Campaign 2009).

Since many activists and apparel businesses are deadlocked on whether minimum or living wages should be set as standards for social responsibility, some organizations are looking for alternative methods for ensuring wages for apparel workers are improved over time. The Fair Wear Foundation (FWF) is incorporating a fair wage ladder into its audits of apparel factories. The wage ladder provides a means of visually tracking factory wages over time by depicting on a ladder-like scale different wage levels and standards set for a particular region or country, along with a particular factory's wage average. According to Henrik Lindholm (2009), International Verification Coordinator for the FWF, how to remediate wages that are too low or stagnant remains to be determined; however, the wage ladder is a basis for workers to discuss wages with management.

In an initiative more geared toward small producers and home workers, a Fair Wage Guide developed by World of Good seeks to assist fair trade artisans and buyers in identifying fair wages and prices for handicrafts. The online calculator allows inputs of country of production (also state), skill level of the artisan (high or unskilled), how much they are paid per piece, how much time is taken to complete one piece, and whether the artisan has to pay for the materials (www.fairtradecalculator.com) and the output evaluates whether the wages meet minimum and living wage standards. World of Good reports that by using the guide, 320 cooperatives in sixty-one countries have improved their bargaining power when negotiating wages. The systemic nature of very low wages has been confirmed in India, where between 2006 and 2008, 35 percent of 15,670 home workers in the craft sector were making under the local minimum wage (Silverman 2009).

Although the calculator reportedly increases the bargaining power of cooperative businesses, one fair trade handicraft buyer we have talked with indicates,

> The calculator has lost credibility with suppliers who see it as overly critical of their good intentions . . . the mere presence of a standardized "calculator" seems to cause a level of defensiveness and emphasize the existence of an unequal power relationship. As a result, the calculator has in many cases eroded trust and taken power away from the hands of the very people whom it was intended to empower. (Personal communication with a fair trade buyer 2008)

The buyer explains further by sharing an e-mail she had received from one fair trade producer.

> To imply the groups who can't pay 78 [Indian rupees] a day on average should feel ashamed to exist . . . sounds patronizing. If "encouragement" turns into pressure to pay such and such amount when the group is really trying, then the balance shifts into "you know more than us" and the dialogue stops. (Personal communication with a fair trade buyer 2008)

Vaughan-Whitehead (2009) encourages using multiple dimensions for measuring progress on wages, explaining that

> The payment of "fair wages" should ensure workers decent living standards but also other key basic conditions within their company, such as the payment of the minimum wage and other legal benefits (social contributions; paid holidays and so on), no excessive working hours and the regular payment of wages and benefits. It should also make sure that no alienating wage fixing systems prevail—dominated by, for instance, wage sanctions or unbalanced use of piece rates—and that they are not unilaterally decided by the employer without any communication channel and individual and collective bargaining. At the same time, workers should be ensured . . . that their wages will be regularly adjusted to price increases, provide a share of their enterprise's performance, and also reflect changes in work intensity, technology and human capital. (32)

The draft standard for apparel certification issued by Transfair USA (2009) requires that at a minimum, workers are paid the legal wage or one determined through collective bargaining. From that basis, wages must be gradually improved to living wage levels. The fair trade premium paid beyond wages for worker groups to determine distribution will slide between 1 and 10 percent, with the highest premiums required when minimum wages are paid. The debate on how best to ensure fair wages informed our analysis of the income generated by women working with MarketPlace. We calculated a living wage and gathered minimum wage data, using these data points to determine how MarketPlace wages stacked up against these standards.

While a fair trade apparel certification program may represent progress in that it could allow handicraft producers to have garments they produce certified as meeting fair trade standards, the program being piloted by Transfair USA seems to advantage large producers in industrial settings over small producer organizations engaged in handicraft production methods. It is unclear whether the clothing and household goods produced by the women working with MarketPlace could meet these newly developed standards. Would other certification programs be more appropriate for 100% Fair Trade organizations?

Fair Trade Certification for Small Producers and Handicrafts

Given the changes marking fair trade over the last ten or more years, it is not surprising that there is growing tension within the movement. Organizations that started fair trade and remain focused on building and strengthening relationships with small farmers and artisan producers espouse different goals than the labeling initiatives and corporations that have more recently become involved and aim to increase sales of fair trade products. The certification of fair trade agricultural products has marginalized small producers and farmers as well as a whole range of products, including handicrafts (Keahey, Littrell, and Murray forthcoming; Nicholls and Opal 2005).

The World Fair Trade Organization (WFTO, renamed from IFAT (International Federation of Alternative Trade) in 2009) makes clear that it distinguishes fair trade and ethical trade being practiced by large-scale businesses such as those in the apparel industry, indicating that

> Fair Trade is about more than following codes of conduct and meeting labour standards. Fair Trade organisations specifically seek to work in partnership with marginalised and disadvantaged groups to try and help them overcome the serious barriers they face in finding markets. Therefore, while a Fair Trade business must be ethical, an ethical business is not necessarily Fair Trade. (WFTO, *Frequently Asked Questions* 2009)

As with commodity fair traders, handicraft organizations have faced questions of accountability for their practices. The product certification system developed by FLO for agricultural commodities did not apply to handicrafts and did not always work well for small agricultural producers. The emerging certification of fair trade apparel and home goods likewise seems not to fully address the needs of small producers who are engaged in fair trade. A program created by the WFTO may fill this need.

In 2004, the WFTO, with its significant membership of handicraft enterprises in developing countries, created an organizational monitoring system for small producer groups and retailers (WFTO, *Monitoring* 2009). The WFTO's *Ten Standards of Fair Trade* (2009) are elements for measurement (see Table 2.3), and are accompanied by indicators for entry level and progressive level compliance.

Producers submit a self-assessment with supporting documentation that demonstrates commitment to the WFTO's standards whereupon a monitoring department scores the applicant and provides feedback on actions needed for compliance. Applicant organizations attaining a certain level of compliance against the standards become approved member fair trade organizations and are allowed to use the WFTO logo that confirms their demonstrated 100 percent commitment to fair trade across all of the

Table 2.3 WFTO Ten Standards of Fair Trade

PRINCIPLE	EXPLANATION
Creating opportunities for economically disadvantaged producers	Create opportunities for producers who have been economically disadvantaged or marginalized by the conventional trading system
Transparency and accountability	Transparent management and commercial relations with trading partners
Capacity building	Develop producers' independence. Provide continuity of trade during which management skills are increased and new markets accessed
Promoting fair trade	Provide customers with information about the organization, products, and how they were made. High standards of product quality and packing
Payment of a fair price	Pay a fair price in the local context. Cover the cost of production that is environmentally and socially sound. Provide equal pay for equal work of men and women. Prompt payment and access to preproduction or harvest financing
Gender equity	Women's work is properly recognized, valued, and rewarded
Working conditions	Safe and healthy working environment. Children's participation (if any) does not adversely affect their well-being, security, education, and need for play
Child labor	Respect the UN Convention on the Rights of the Child as well as local laws and norms that ensure working conditions outlined above
The environment	Encourage better environmental practices and the application of responsible methods of production
Trade relations	Display concern for the social, economic, and environmental well-being of marginalized small producers and do not maximize profit at their expense. Maintain long-term relationships based on solidarity, trust, and mutual respect

Note: Adapted from *Ten Standards of Fair Trade* (WFTO, 2009).

organization's work (WFTO, *Marks and Labels* 2009; WFTO, *Monitoring* 2009). As the WFTO states,

> WFTO members are organisations differentiated by their 100% Fair Trade commitment to eradicate poverty through sustainable economic development; pioneering social and environmental policy

and practice and continual reinvestment in marginalised artisans, farmers and producer communities in some of the most fragile places on earth. (WFTO, *The World Fair Trade Organization* 2009)

With the WFTOs organizational emphasis, the term "alternative trading organization," which had been less frequently used over the last decade, was now replaced with the reference "100% Fair Trade."

Only a small number of producers have been randomly audited to verify their compliance since the 100% Fair Trade program began (Paul Myers, personal communication August 2009). Recognizing the shortcomings of this, WFTO in 2009 was developing a second stage of certification and accountability involving independent third party certification for organizations demonstrating fair trade practices in all of their business activities. The Sustainable Fair Trade Management System (SFTMS) is aimed especially at small- and medium-sized organizations that could not meet, or choose not to pursue, FLO certification. In order to demonstrate compliance, organizations must publicly commit to adhering to the SFTMS principles and comply with those principles, demonstrate through third-party verification by a WFTO-accredited auditor that they have practices and procedures that support the principles, and communicate the results of third-party verification to the public. Fair trade organizations of both handicrafts and commodities, once certified through third party review, will be able to use the SFTMS label on all their products (WFTO, *SFTMS* 2009). Fair trade movement leader and president of the WFTO, Paul Myers, believes that by creating compatible fair trade marks, FLO and the WFTO are reunifying the commodity and handicraft sectors and strengthening fair trade governance (personal communication August 2009).

While the apparel and household goods produced by the women working with MarketPlace had not been covered under the national labeling initiatives and FLO, and may not be certified under the new initiative being launched by Transfair USA, the new WFTO organizational certification for 100% Fair Trade would apply since it focuses on organizations versus specific products. If so, this promising development would allow fair trade as originally envisioned to be continued and respected in the market.

Ensuring Fair Trade Is Decent Work

Current debate about fair trade apparel certification by fair trade leaders, labor activists, and others has closely connected fair trade and CSR as practiced in the global apparel industry by large corporate brands and retailers. In contrast, the WFTO's organizational certification emphasizes the realities of small- and medium-sized organizations with income-generating and development-focused goals. Although the TransFair USA apparel certification may appear more rigorous than the WFTO's certification by explicitly connecting its standards to the ILO's Fundamental Principles and Rights at Work, the WFTO organizational certification of fair trade need not be viewed as lacking. Whether it is practiced in large or small production sites, with or without corporations, and certified or not, there is at least implicit agreement across both certification programs that fair trade must provide decent work. The ILO defines that "decent work sums up the aspirations of people in their working lives—their aspirations for opportunity and income; rights, voice and recognition; family stability and personal development; and fairness and gender equality" (International Labour Organization, *Decent Work for All*). Decent work involves all workers being able to attain basic worker rights, "the basic rights at work of a worker are internationally recognized human rights. Human rights are indivisible and have to be applied to everyone" (ILO 2007, 38). Achieving decent work is relevant to all workers and should be considered in both industrial work settings and development projects.

There are many aspects of decent work and human rights that clearly align with the WFTO's fair trade mission, including the following:

- Helping individuals obtain life skills that will assist them in obtaining work

- Preventing discrimination

- Promoting safety at work

- Increasing women's participation in work

- Providing skills training meeting the demands of the labor market

- Involving workers' organizations and employers in designing training programs

- Creating opportunities to increase income-earning capacity of specific disadvantaged or marginalized groups, including informal workers, people in rural areas, poor women, people with disabilities, and others

- Helping people be citizens, and enhance their culture, education, family, and community, etc., and thus more holistically enhance their lives throughout their lifecycle

- Providing fair wages (ILO 2007)

Strategies for achieving decent work and human rights need to be customized for each country and each level of development; benchmarks need to be developed and data gathered in order to show accountability for upholding those rights.

> A human-rights–based approach focuses on the realization of the rights of the excluded and marginalized populations, and those whose rights are at risk of being violated, building on the premise that a country cannot achieve sustained progress without recognizing human rights principles (especially universality) as core principles of governance. Universality means that all people have human rights, even if resource constraints imply prioritization. It does *not* mean that all problems of all people must be tackled at once. (Office of the United Nations High Commissioner for Human Rights 2006, 16)

Literature outlining the trajectory of fair trade of agricultural commodities and reports of new debates about certifying fair trade apparel frame our analysis of the emerging opportunities and threats for workers engaged in fair trade production of garments and handicrafts. In presenting and discussing our findings, we assess how fair trade apparel certification and WFTO organizational certification may impact workers who sew and embroider for MarketPlace. By profiling how these workers have been empowered by the development activities of a 100% Fair Trade organization, we are able to consider the importance of a fair trade model that holds holistic development as a core value. Knowing of a growing division within the fair trade movement, we are drawn to consider how a fair trade model focused on economic growth and market expansion and that includes corporate retailers and large-scale production might also retain a dual focus on the more difficult to measure social benefits of fair trade. Likewise, an understanding of the need to explicitly and progressively work to uphold all individuals' human and worker rights helps us evaluate whether 100% Fair Trade might be strengthened for further empowerment of the women whose lives we detail.

Artisan Enterprises

Handicrafts join with dance, music, writing, and architecture to form a larger category called cultural industries, or "those aspects of a culture that can form the basis of a marketable product" (Liebl 2005). UNESCO (United Nations Educational, Scientific and Cultural Organization), the United

Nations agency with a specific mandate for culture, offers a more extended definition.

> Cultural industries are defined as those industries which produce tangible or intangible artistic and creative outputs, and have a potential for wealth creation and income generation through the exploitation of culture assets and production of knowledge-based goods and services (both traditional and contemporary). What cultural industries have in common is that they all use creativity, cultural knowledge and intellectual property to produce goods and services with social and cultural impact. (Askerud and Englehardt 2007, 11)

This definition acknowledges the international community's recognition of the role of culture and cultural industries in development. In South and Southeast Asia, this recognition has been further supported through international organizations and agencies. Conferences and symposia have brought together planners, consultants, and scholars to assess the status of various cultural industries, including handicrafts; to address global appropriation of intellectual property held in these industries; and to propose strategies for growth through national, tourist, and export markets.[1] Askerud and Englehardt (2007) conclude,

> What remains now is for governments to adopt policy measures to activate this new-found understanding of the role of culture in development. To do so, and to make informed decisions which will successfully promote cultural industries, reliable data and meaningful statistics are required. (iv)

A goal of this book is to paint a reliable research picture that can inform governmental decisions on support of cultural industries.

As background, in this section we draw from symposia papers and selected publications to provide an overview of issues and challenges within the craft sector in India. A broader context for the issues beyond India is offered where support is available. Finally, some encouraging initiatives underway for craft development and enterprise sustainability are introduced.

Artisans in India: Issues and Challenges

Despite the impressive growth in the Indian handicraft sector introduced in Chapter 1, Maureen Liebl (2005), a longtime crafts administrator, scholar, and consultant in India, offers a reminder of the daily life faced by craftspersons.

> The majority of craftspersons in India still live lives that are far from ideal, that much too small a percentage of the industry's earnings reaches the actual producers, that policy needs are immense, and that economic gain has been offset, at least to some extent, by loss of meaning and integrity of form.

Yet, despite this picture, Ashoke Chatterjee (2007), a leader of craft development in India, projects that "crafts offer India the only sustainable answer to its need of job opportunities for a population that has crossed one billion" (12). Acknowledging that not all traditional skills offer economic viability, development planners face difficult choices for directing their limited resources. Focusing on those artisans who have unrealized potential to jointly generate income and preserve a culturally precious artistic resource seems most worthy of attention. For these artisans, income generation serves as a precursor to cultural asset protection (Liebl and Roy 2004).

In their everyday lives, artisans face a variety of conditions arising from and contributing to poverty. The majority of artisans are of castes and social classes that have precluded them from opportunities for education and whose exposure beyond their rural communities is limited. Many artisans, as informal sector workers in their homes, are dependent on agents to provide orders that can vary widely across the year and be subject to agents' manipulative whims (Wilkinson-Weber 1999). Artisans experience asymmetry of information about the market as contrasted with middlemen who exploit their sales (Liebl and Roy 2003). For women in Muslim communities that follow female seclusion and sexual segregation practices, market ignorance prevails (Wilkinson-Weber 1999). Price spreads between the retail price and the price paid to the artisan can be enormous. As an example, study of a craft product in the Jodhpur export market revealed a ratio as high as seventy to one between retailer and craftsperson, with many middlemen profiting along the way (Liebl and Roy 2004).

Despite market differentials, Wilkinson-Weber (1999) notes from her in-depth study of the chikan embroidery industry in Lucknow that income from embroidery should not be considered inconsequential. Rather, it is the only income among Muslim women with few other job alternatives. Embroidery work is most certainly not a pastime to fill empty hours.

> The prevalent description of chikan embroidery as "free-time" labor distorts the true circumstances of embroiderers' lives. The implication

is that they have empty, leisure time in which to do some extra work and that filling these hours with work for wages is a matter of simple, personal choice. But women do not have much time in which they have nothing better to do, and it is not out of choice but from necessity that they do chikan. (120)

While MarketPlace, the focus of this book, is not about self-employed women in the informal sector economy, some attention to the conditions for self-employed artisans is warranted, given the vast numbers of artisans in informal work. In particular, SEWA's observations from working with artisans provide some comparative examples for the MarketPlace fair trade organizational approach. As SEWA began working with embroiderers in rural Kachcch, an area where over 80 percent of the women possess embroidery skills, they observed the women's anxiety about generating income. Ela Bhatt (2006) described,

> The traders are well aware of the women's desperation to sell, while the women do not have the economic cushion to wait for a better price. At the back of their minds is the fear: "What if the next trader never comes? What if he doesn't come soon enough? What will I do?" Ready cash is of unparalleled value in tough times. And their embroideries have good cash value. (147)

As SEWA worked with the women to establish an organizational structure for their sales, leaders described conditions of constraint that the women faced (Bhatt 2006). Women felt resistance from their communities for travel to the office for sales or to cities for exhibition. Resistance was fueled by community speculation as to what women were doing when they "roamed around on their own" (151). Women who had always been on the receiving end of directions, primarily from male family members, had little experience in taking initiative. Lack of time management skills in activities beyond the household led women to take on orders which they could not complete for time-bound export shipments; fear of unemployment drove the women's unrealistic acceptance of orders. While the women came to recognize the need to produce for market demand, they also expressed that their creative process of embroidery was stifled as their products became homogenized for an urban market. Occasionally, out of frustration, an embroiderer would insert a few bright stitches to appease her aesthetic; however, this usually led to sales rejection.

In a final condition impacting artisans, within the textile segment of the crafts sector, many weavers, embroiderers, and dyers have watched their local markets evaporate as clothing preferences change. Older Indian women select less expensive, machine-woven saris over exquisite hand-woven products. Younger women turn to western attire or salwar kamiz, with few classic, Indian, surface embellishments (Liebl and Roy 2004). Textiles, and other Indian crafts as well, are losing out to mass-produced alternatives in the form of cheap "plagiarized" imports, many from China (Chatterjee 2007). Expanding to national, tourist, and export markets offers an alternative. However, Chatterjee (2007) warns that a critical mindset must change for success to occur; "India persists in promoting its crafts with, 'This is what we make, please buy it' rather than a confident 'We know what you need and we can supply it' stance" (12).

Major issues emerge for artisans when they turn their attention to external markets about which they have limited market knowledge. Among the challenges they face are amplified production expectations. External wholesale buyers within India and from abroad demand higher, exacting quality and increased production capacity achieved through more efficient, timely, and labor-saving processes. Product standardization is often a novel concept for artisans who have previously customized their production for individual local patrons.

A second issue involves new product innovation. Long-used methods of intergenerational transfer of skills learned through repeated copying of designs do not offer encouragement for infusion of new design and product ideas. Within India, Liebl and Roy (2004) note that "copying has never had the pejorative connotations that it does in the West. Rather, the most important task of the artist is seen to be the interpretation of a classic theme, rather than the creation of a new one" (61). Design ownership is seldom acknowledged. Yet, external design consultants, with whom artisans collaborate, likely bring differing perspectives on innovation and design as intellectual property. The resolution of design ownership, copying versus innovation, and the appropriation of creativity will call for careful intra- and intercultural negotiation. It is hoped that in the process, Indian designs and skills do not become so "decontextualized" and "trivialized" in form that they hold little meaning for the artisans (Liebl 2005).

In a third issue, how technical and design training is conducted will be critical for its acceptance and application. Attention to teaching methods that match learning styles within artisan communities seems particularly crucial given the learning-by-intergenerational-copying approach that is common in India and the perspective that a slight change represents innovation. Aid to Artisans (ATA), a global leader in artisan enterprise training and development, notes the variance in teaching styles that they have incorporated around the world. Clare Smith, former President of ATA, cites the need for trainers to attend to artisans' expectations for demonstrations, teaching aids, and interactional formality and to their receptivity to and definition of innovation (Clare Smith, personal communication 1998).

In another issue, whether artisan groups can move toward Chatterjee's "we know what you need and can supply it" stance will be constrained by their ability to acquire the necessary working capital to purchase equipment for expanding production capacity and to garner credit or loans to keep their production afloat while orders are filled. As Liebl and Roy (2004) note,

> The producer who receives a large order will often not be able to find the funds necessary to purchase raw material in bulk, or to support the family while the work is in process. And the irony is that the amounts that could make a real difference to the crafts producer are often extremely modest. Various credit schemes are available to craftspeople, primarily through government institutions, but it is difficult for the uneducated artisan to understand and access these programs, and it is often impossible for a poor craftsperson to manage the necessary collateral or funds for required bribes. (59)

Finally, enterprise leaders play a critical role for a group's success in making the necessary changes to meet the demand of external markets. Across her years of observing and working with Indian artisan groups, Liebl (2005) notes the "individual-driven development of many cultural industries." When that visionary and motivated leadership is not institutionalized in the organization, the enterprise tends to collapse upon the leader's departure. The vital role of visionary and often selfless leaders is supported around the world. In an analysis of successful artisan projects assisted by ATA, enterprise leaders were charismatic, entrepreneurial, risk takers, highly respected within the group, and well-connected in their communities (Cockram 2005; Gottschling, Littrell, and Cockram 2005; Littrell, Cockram, and Strawn 2005a, 2005b). In another study, among seventeen US Peace Corps-assisted handicraft groups in eleven countries, enterprise leaders exhibited a clear sense of purpose, strong organizational skills and represented a "centrifugal force from which a producer group gained collective strength and action. Facilitators' sense of purpose planted seeds for developing self-confidence and authority among craft producers" (Durham and Littrell 2000, 266).

Indian Initiatives for Artisan Enterprise Sustainability

Despite the challenges faced by artisans in producing for external markets, three examples provide evidence of successful Indian artisan collaborations. One flourishing firm of long standing is Jaipur-based Anokhi. Block-printed fabrics and vegetable-dyed fabrics are hallmarks of the Anokhi apparel and housewares lines that are marketed domestically and abroad (Anokhi, 2009). Faith and J. (John) Singh founded Anokhi over thirty years ago to prove that "it is possible to run a successful craft-based business using traditional techniques to meet contemporary tastes, thus ensuring that the craft lives on while providing a livelihood for the men and women involved in the craft" (Radhakrishnan 2003). Business values of fair trade, openness, and taking care of people guided the company.

Block printing of Anokhi fabrics is decentralized in villages around Jaipur, with the company headquarters located on a farm just outside Jaipur. Following in-house designing, fabrics, dyes, and wood blocks are transported to the artisans who print in their homes. Pritam Singh, son of Faith and John and the company's current managing director, elaborates,

> This decentralized system of hand block-printing involves the efforts of over 1000 craftsmen and helps them work in conditions of their own choosing while, at the same time, providing them with the security of regular work. In fact, creating a safety net for everyone associated—both directly and indirectly—with the company is almost an obsession with the management.

Because block printing is viewed as a man's craft in India, Anokhi has also attended to the needs of rural women. Women's groups provide embroidery and others work at the manufacturing plant located at the farm outside Jaipur. Social services for all employees include healthcare benefits, a daycare at the factory, and educational support for children. While many people have been involved over the years in Anokhi's evolution, Liebl and Roy (2004) assess that a crucial element has been the personal commitment and passion on the part of the firm's founders and current leaders.

A second example, the Kala Raksha Vidhyalaya design school, provides education "gauged to move those who produce centuries old traditional crafts from artisans who merely fulfill orders, to designers who influence the market" (Misha Black Award 2009). An arm of the Kala Raksha artisan group in Kutch, the school embodies a dream of Kala Rasksha Director Judy Frater to provide design education for artisans involved in block printing and embroidery. Because artisans find it difficult to leave their homes for long periods of time, the yearlong course is divided into six shorter units spread across a year.

Twenty-five to thirty students, in separate groups of men and women that conform to local social norms, travel to the residential school located along the gulf of Kutch for intense study over one- to two-week periods. In addition to the classroom lectures, discussions, and demonstrations, a CAD (computer-aided design) lab and a library of historic textiles provide resources for design experimentation and inspiration. Course units, taught by visiting design educators from India and abroad, include (1) Color: Sourcing from heritage and nature, (2) Basic design: Sourcing from heritage and nature, (3) Market orientation, (4) Concept, communication, and projects, (5). Finishing and collection development, and (6) Presentation (Kala Raksha Vidylaya: An institution of design for traditional artisans 2009). Each student develops a final design collection that is juried by a panel of eminent Indian craft experts. In a statement of support for Frater's 2009 Sir Misha Black Medal for Distinguished Services to Design Education, Ashoke Chatterjee described,

> Nothing like this has ever happened before—it is the first effort of its kind anywhere in the world; a design school tailored to the needs and capacities of a local community of artists using this as a force for strengthening craft diversity, as distinct from diluting tradition through training unrelated to a community or culture. It offers a genuine context for re-vitalizing craft tradition in a contemporary setting—it provides a process of learning that goes beyond literacy. (Misha Black Awards 2009)

A final example introduces the next generation of India's fashion designers to collaboration with rural artisans on new product development. The National Institute of Fashion Technology (NIFT), India's premier higher education institution offering bachelor's degrees in apparel design, involves students in a crafts cluster sequence of activities during their third year of studies. Student teams travel to a group of rural villages to study a cluster of crafts in media such as textiles, leather, wood, ceramics, and metal. Through in-depth interviews and observations with the artisans, students document the craft's history and tradition in well-illustrated books that become part of the NIFT design repository. Upon return to campus, the students transition the crafts to new products for domestic markets, primarily in urban areas. In a third stage, artisans from the villages come to one of the twelve NIFT campuses, set up their equipment, and work with the students to produce the students' designs. In this final stage, students and artisans negotiate value-added changes that fit the artisans' traditions and meet market demand (Vandana Bhandari, personal communication October 1, 2009).

Artisan Enterprise Beyond India: Lessons Learned

A series of artisan enterprise case studies developed by ATA provides lessons learned that are useful for comparative assessment with our MarketPlace analysis (Cockram 2005; Gottschling, Littrell, and Cockram 2005; Littrell, Cockram, and Strawn 2005a, 2005b). ATA, an internationally recognized and active development organization, typically works with artisan groups on time- and funding-limited interventions of three to five years. Goals center on product development for export markets of handicrafts. In 2004-2005, the Ford Foundation funded follow-up assessment of projects for which external funding had ceased for at least three years in Armenia, Central Asia, Ghana, Honduras, Hungary, Peru, and Russia.

Lessons learned from successful projects and relevant to this book related to characteristics of the leaders, the artisans' cultural context and attitudes toward learning, and work patterns. Leaders of successful projects exhibited strong entrepreneurial drive and problem-solving ability. They were aware that growth required frequent reinvention of products and processes; yet, they were also mindful that new product design must take production limitations into account. The most successful projects evolved among artisans who had few employment options and who sought creative and interesting work. Artisans were willing to adapt business practices and products to meet current trends among their customers. Despite intervention from ATA, artisan work was often part-time and seasonal.

Within successful ATA supported artisan groups, best practices evolved that brought artisan groups together to learn from each other. Teaching of artisan-generated innovation was considered central to training for the increasingly competitive global market. By participating in local sales opportunities among the expat community, successful artisan groups vetted new products and gained valuable feedback by visiting with customers.

This overview of the artisan sector in India and beyond calls attention to the urgent need for organizational models for cultural enterprises that can lead to sustainability in meeting the demands of external markets while retaining craft design and procedural integrity. Scholars, consultants, and development planners point to specific handicraft sector challenges for comparison and contrast with MarketPlace's growth.

Conclusions

Each of the three bodies of scholarship provided unique frames for our analysis of MarketPlace artisans. Development scholars challenged us to explore the lives of artisans both holistically in terms of capabilities, livelihood, and well-being, as well as to look closely at how capabilities, agency, social recognition, and personal confidence are interrelated in MarketPlace's dual model of profit generation and human empowerment. The draft standard for fair trade apparel and home goods certification issued by Transfair USA and WFTO Ten Standards of Fair Trade provided benchmarks for examining MarketPlace's practices in contributing to impact social and economic change. Finally, the issues and challenges characterizing Indian artisans offered a context for comparative assessment of MarketPlace within the larger framework of cultural industries in India.

Note

1. Examples of conferences include *Asia-Pacific Creative Communities: A Strategy for the 21st Century Senior Expert Symposium,* UNESCO, Jodhpur, India, February 2005; Asia *Cultural Cooperation Forum on Measuring Creativity, Happiness and Well-Being,* UNESCO, November 2006.

CHAPTER 3

The MarketPlace Story

Compared with millions of women in India, Pushpika Freitas, founder of MarketPlace: Handwork of India, experienced a privileged childhood. With six daughters, Francis and Florentina (Flory) Freitas did not have a lot of money for luxuries, or even the bare necessities at times. The family faced day-to-day challenges as part of India's struggling middle class. Pushpika recalls her mother often saying that the family was a hairbreadth away from living in the slums because of their lack of money. Yet, Pushpika's mother and father were progressive and the girls were all brought up to be independent. Through dinner and bedtime conversations, the girls learned that everyone's views counted and household decisions were made democratically.

Pushpika's mother served as a strong role model for her daughters in encouraging community involvement and promoting education. Even with little money, Flory Freitas always did some kind of social work—collecting money for the Catholic church or convent or for a home for street children. When Pushpika's mother was in her late fifties, she attended a neighbor's party where a physician was talking about the terrible physical and social consequences of leprosy. Flory immediately responded, "Let's do something about it."

At that time in the mid-1970s, the Indian government, volunteer organizations, and the World Health Organization had programs to identify and treat leprosy patients. Detection and treatment in the early stages of leprosy was relatively easy. However, those who had contracted leprosy were stigmatized by society and did not necessarily seek initial treatment or rehabilitation. To begin her leprosy work, Pushpika's mother joined with Catholic nuns, helping them raise money for leprosy patients in Mumbai. When a German foundation contributed the necessary funding for leprosy programming in Mumbai, Flory Freitas shifted her efforts to the organization's medical agenda. By 1980 and within just five years of its formation, Maharashtra Lokahita Seva Mandal (Helping the people of Maharashtra) treated 10,000 leprosy patients in Mumbai.

Pushpika's parents were also influential because of the emphasis they placed on education for their daughters. From an early age, Pushpika and her sisters knew they were bound for college. Pushpika's mother had grown up in a family that did not prioritize education for women; however, her father held a different perspective for women's instruction. Pushpika's mother had attained a high school education and her mother's younger sister in Goa would have stopped her education there as well had it not been for Pushpika's father who convinced his father-in-law that the younger sister should be educated beyond high school. Further stressing the importance of education, as Pushpika was growing up, her mother would emphasize to her daughters that beauty did not really mean anything. Rather it was what you are inside and how you used your knowledge that was important.

To her parent's dismay, Pushpika was not a very good student—at least when it came to the rote memorization required at the lower levels of schooling in India. But when Pushpika enrolled at the School of Social Work in the University of Bombay, she began to excel in response to more diverse pedagogical methods. After completing a bachelor's degree in social work, Pushpika traveled to the United States, where she pursued a master's degree in sociology at DePaul University in Chicago, Illinois.

Once she completed her graduate degree in 1980, Pushpika returned home to follow her mother by initiating a leprosy rehabilitation program in Mumbai. Whereas her mother's organization focused on medical treatment for leprosy, Pushpika directed her attention toward rehabilitation among individuals with disabilities resulting from the disease. Living in leprosy colonies, residents were exploited to make illegal liquor for outsiders who were alert that police would not venture into the neighborhoods. As a result, alcoholism was very high among those living in the colonies. The German foundation funding Pushpika's mother's program wanted to start a microenterprise loan program to initiate work alternatives. Pushpika joined their efforts by providing small loans to men under a microenterprise model. While there was some progress, ultimately the project did not have the impact she desired. The men believed that they should not have to pay back the loans since they had leprosy. The men judged that society owed them something due to the stigma they experienced.

Pushpika was frustrated by the lack of innovative thinking about how to establish self-sufficiency. Looking for new ways to provide assistance, Pushpika began to focus more on women and their needs. Talking to women turned out to be an eye-opening experience for Pushpika. By then aged in her mid-twenties, Pushpika had more in common with women who had grown up in Illinois than in India—she had no concept that women often had no control over their lives. Through her discussions, she learned that many women were working hard to keep their families afloat; yet, most had a difficult time making ends meet. While women in general were at the bottom of the social hierarchy with absolutely zero advantages, Pushpika realized that the widows with whom she talked were in even more vulnerable positions.

For those women with husbands, the men were frequently unemployed. Physical and mental abuse from husbands was common. A visitor to Pushpika's home cemented her commitment to working with women. Pushpika recalls,

> Late one evening a woman came to my house and asked, "Pushpika, can I leave this stove with you because my husband is drunk and he's going to sell it and it will take months to save enough money to buy a new one, so can you keep it for me for a couple of days?" That was when it hit me that women had so little control over their lives. A woman is defined by her relationship to a man. And although she may be the sole breadwinner in the family, she still has no decision-making power to say that their daughter should go to school or how many children they should have, nothing. It just didn't seem fair.

Women who could find employment often worked as maids in homes where they were treated like servants. Women were required to work when they were sick and felt demeaned by their employers who believed the women were poor because they wanted to be poor, lacked ambition, or were lazy. By the time that Pushpika learned of their plight, the women were eager to do almost anything to improve their situations.

Like her mother, who had decided on the spur of the moment to take action when she learned of leprosy problems, Pushpika did not spend time thinking about how to solve the women's employment problems nor what sort of impact a solution might have. Instead, she said "let's just try something." With the support of her mother and sisters, Pushpika started working with three women. The women gathered at a leprosy clinic and began sewing patchwork quilts by hand as they didn't know how to use a machine. Pushpika recalls,

> When I began working with women in the slums of Mumbai in 1980 I had no idea what I was doing. I did, however, quickly realize that I was very fortunate. I could not understand why the women I met in the slums not only lacked rights and were treated terribly, but they did not expect anything different. I learned that they had no options, so this became the first goal of Marketplace; to provide them with an opportunity, the chance to earn a dignified living.

Self-sufficiency Versus Charity

From MarketPlace's inception, Pushpika acted on a philosophy to foster dignity among the women rather than to provide charity. Pushpika believed that self-sufficiency would follow. This approach countered the prevailing social work model at the time where people in need were recipients of charitable aid. Incipient impressions formed during her early years contributed to Pushpika's evolving approach to working with women. As a child, Pushpika remembers that people would donate eggs for tuberculosis (TB) patients. She and her sisters would go to collect the eggs early in the morning, boil them, and then hand them out to the TB patients who would come to their front door. Pushpika did not believe that charity was always bad, but she would sometimes tease her mother that if a woman cried about her life's miseries for half an hour, she was given 1,000 rupees, and if she cried for an hour, she got 5,000 rupees. Pushpika had been influenced by her mother's great empathy for people and she wanted to dedicate her life to helping, but she aspired to try an alternative approach. With a firm commitment to self-sufficiency and not to charity, Pushpika, along with her sister Lalita and three women from the slums, began the work that would evolve into MarketPlace. The women, one widow and two married individuals, from the slums had no income at the time. All had small children.

Interested in expanding their work to include other women, from the start the sisters asked the members themselves to evaluate whether another potential woman should be part of the group. The original trio of women would visit the home of a prospective participant and come back with an assessment. Part of their evaluation involved looking at the available family resources. A widowed woman with three children had higher priority than someone with a twenty-one-year-old son who was not employed but had the potential to be working. Pushpika remembers that one woman who had a television and a son in Dubai was not accepted into the group. While she was not wealthy, there were others who were poorer and exhibited greater need.

Beyond Economic Empowerment

While Pushpika's fledgling organization initially focused on economic empowerment, the next step centered on building leadership to run the emerging business.

> When we started work in Mumbai in 1980 our primary goal was to
> provide women with opportunities to earn a dignified living, reach

their potential, and redesign the destinies of their children. We were not propelled by any particular theoretical principles of development. Without knowing it, we were driven by the compulsion to empower women.

After bringing together an initial group of women, the enterprise members began to focus on spotting leadership potential to run the business of sewing patchwork quilts. Initially, no one among the poor whom they were helping had ever worked in an office. A vital prerequisite was that the woman needed to be allowed out of the house to work in the office. While this simple criterion might have surprised some Westerners, many Indian women from the slums were confined to their homes either because of the considerable housework, for religious reasons, or because the husband and in-laws with whom the woman lived did not believe that women should be active outside the home. As Pushpika and others looked for potential leaders, they recognized that some characteristics went hand in hand—women who really wanted to work and make something of themselves also exhibited incipient leadership qualities. Because there were already a number of charity-based organizations for leprosy patients to turn to, Pushpika's group looked for women who were drawing on other, non–charity-based resources to get by.

MarketPlace centered their efforts with women because there was such need and women had a strong desire to work. The men in the families where women could leave the home to work generally went along with the effort since the women were able to carry out the household tasks they normally did, such as cooking, tending children, and fetching water, along with their income generation through sewing. As well, economic improvement was a topic that husbands and wives could agree was needed.

As Pushpika and Lalita listened to the women, they heard the priority that the women voiced for education. Some of the educational needs were quite simple. Women wanted to learn how to write their names so they could sign their children's report cards from school, and to learn numbers so they could read the bus signs. Pushpika was shocked, realizing she would never have thought about something so basic. She had been thinking of the need for nutrition education, but the women said, "Forget it, we know how to cook," which was something that Pushpika did not know how to do. Her initial lack of understanding of the women's most basic needs sparked Pushpika's commitment to always involve the women in identifying and solving problems within the business. This democratic approach would become a bedrock for social action projects that would build greater self-confidence among the women and expand the impacts of the work to their communities. Pushpika reflects back on MarketPlace's nearly three decades as she discusses the leadership that has emerged when women's needs are acknowledged and addressed from within the group.

> What moves me every time I visit India and the various groups is the energy and enthusiasm of the women. In 1980, I never dreamed of these changes, these developments and these successes. The leadership that has emerged over the years has been amazing. Women have been able to assume these newfound roles without upsetting the family structure. They have taken up learning computers with such zeal and without the slightest inhibition, and they have assumed leadership roles like they were born with them. They have collaborated and disagreed but always kept the group welfare in mind when resolving conflict.

Early Business Activity

Pushpika and Lalita's initial involvement with the women in 1982 and 1983 involved patchwork, using hand-sewing skills that the women had learned while growing up. The sisters obtained leftover fabric from tailors, augmented it with some purchased fabric, and taught the women basic patchwork techniques. The group would meet three times a week and the women would take work home, complete the sewing, and then bring it back. Pushpika's mother had some contacts with a French alliance that organized an exhibition before Christmas. The women participated in the sale but were dejected when they sold very few of their patchwork pillow covers during this first marketing venture. Pushpika and Lalita were concerned about the future of the group and were uncertain about what to do next.

The group changed directions from household items to produce clothing because they realized people were willing to spend rupees when they wanted a new kurta or sari. Interested in making one-of-a-kind things, but also recognizing the limited skills of the women, the group started with yokes or borders of patchwork. The women would sew the patchwork and then appliqué the pieces to kurtas. One or two women were constructing the garments, and the sisters worked to ensure that the sewing remained simple. With the clothing styles worn in India, however, this was easy. The straight cuts of many garments did not require darts or other manipulations and also created little fabric waste. Pushpika recalls, "We kept looking at ways to use the skills the women had, so they would not have to invest time in skill development, which would take longer for them to earn a living."

Early Success

Early in the 1980s, Pushpika's older sister, Indira, was living in Evanston, Illinois. Pushpika was eager for a return visit to the United States to see family and friends. She filled her suitcases with skirts, dresses, and pillow covers made by the women, and her sister Indira organized a home party with neighbors and friends. Pushpika clearly remembers that first home party. "People were saying, 'Wow, this is wonderful. This is great.' And we hadn't had that sort of reaction in India. We sold pretty much everything."

Buoyed by the success of the home party, Pushpika returned to India not yet fully conceptualizing that sales in the United States might be a strategy for further growth. In India, she and the women struggled to find places to hold exhibitions of their work. They tried renting a room in an art gallery, but it proved expensive and sales were not strong in the local market. The group experienced a little success with sales to expatriates, but nothing like the luck they had found in the United States. Overall, the local market offered too much competition with India's rich array of exquisite textile products found everywhere.

In 1984, the expanding organization incorporated with the charity commissioner in Mumbai and began calling itself SHARE (Support the Handicapped's Rehabilitation Effort). By then, the group had a stock of hundreds of the easy-to-make yokes. More and more women were learning about the work and wanted to be involved in the income-producing activity. About a year later, Pushpika returned to the United States with more products and met repeated success with sales. While one home party was not enough to sustain the amount of production occurring in India, Pushpika envisioned that US sales might somehow be expanded. Pushpika and her sisters, Lalita and Indira, communicated on nearly a daily basis about how to expand the effort.

While she had studied in the United States, Pushpika met her future husband, David Barnum. David had been to India several times over the ensuing few years and he and Pushpika knew that if they were married, she would need to move to the United States, where he was employed as a university professor. This led Pushpika to begin thinking of starting an organization in the United States that could market the products of the group in India. In 1986, MarketPlace: Handwork of India, the business and marketing arm of the organization was incorporated as a not-for-profit organization and regular home parties were launched in Evanston, Chicago, and Minnesota, David's home state. In the first year of incorporation, MarketPlace grossed about $12,000 in sales. People seemed very willing to buy and organize a home party, including David's mother and sister. Through these home parties, Pushpika met others who hosted parties in Oak Park and Hyde Park, in addition to Evanston.

As a young married couple, Pushpika and David were living in the Lincoln Park area of Chicago, which was a fairly wealthy part of the city. When they tried a home party there, it was not successful based on the products alone. While people could identify with the mission of the organization, in some cases, customers were looking for clothing more closely associated with current fashions. In other parts of the city, all Pushpika had to do was fill the car with boxes, drive to someone's house, pull out the products, and write the invoices as sales mounted. Women hosting the parties would send out the invitations and make snacks, thus eliminating any overhead for MarketPlace marketing. Hostesses coupled the sales with telling the MarketPlace story.

By 1987-1988 and drawing upon the knowledge gained about the customers for MarketPlace's products, Pushpika decided to grow the organization further by initiating a catalog business. Knowing that start-up funding would be required, Pushpika started selling through trade shows, first at the Chicago Apparel Mart. Because they did not have a line of products that could be purchased wholesale, they sold the inventory of one-of-a-kind items on the spot. As well, Pushpika researched how to raise money and wrote seventy-five proposals to potential funders. The results of hard work on proposals paid off when MarketPlace received a grant from the Ford Foundation to develop the work in India and from Catholic Relief Services to launch the catalog business.

No one involved with MarketPlace had any knowledge about the catalog business, so Pushpika was reliant on others for advice. Through a local self-help crafts store, she heard about an upcoming fair trade conference in New Windsor, MD. While attending the conference in 1988, she met Jimmy Pryor from the alternative trading organization, Pueblo to People (see Littrell and Dickson 1999). He and Marty Pole, who was running Deva, another catalog business, proved very helpful to Pushpika, who telephoned frequently to ask, "Now what do I do?"

Pushpika recalls that launching the first catalog was an "absolutely crazy" time and MarketPlace made many mistakes, including not asking for the expiration date on credit cards and having to recontact every customer who had ordered for that information. They had no computers, so everything was done by hand. Yet, sales from the first catalog amounted to $60,000 that allowed them to break even and, with the additional Catholic Relief Services money, continue the effort.

Design and Trade Regulations

Design of the garments evolved along with the growing business. The trade shows helped demonstrate to MarketPlace what was selling and what was not. For example, green garments never sold, emphasizing the importance of color for the US market. Popular clothing at the time in the United States was very loose in comparison to the tight-fitted Indian garments. Sleeves on MarketPlace garments were considered too short for the longer arms of US consumers. According to their US clients, Pushpika learned that women's garments had to have pockets. Because Indian women never wore skirts, getting the length of a skirt right was something MarketPlace had to learn by trial and error. Pushpika describes the evolving designs.

> Partly what I wanted to produce or design were clothes that didn't alienate the producer. So what we've done is take traditional garments and change them around. Like the pants are very traditional but we put pockets in the pants. In India nobody wears their shirt inside or short. The shirt is always long. But here [the U.S.] people would wear them short, so pockets make a good addition.

Besides application of newfound understanding of US women's clothing preferences, another important factor that contributed to design was the importing and quota system. MarketPlace knew they did not want to get involved in export of garments with volume restrictions (quotas) based on bilateral trade agreements because the corruption for obtaining quota was rampant. India's government would open the quota market three or four times per year whereupon groups had to apply. There were two ways to obtain necessary quota—on a first come and first serve basis, or based on the record of exports from the previous year. Bribes to government officials were often involved. They also knew that should they acquire quota, failure to deliver the specified quantity within a specific time frame would result in serious consequences for maintaining the export privilege in ensuing years. MarketPlace feared they were not large or sophisticated enough to compete.

Almost inadvertently, Pushpika heard about India's agreement with the United States for import of traditional Indian garments without quotas. The regulations were workable for MarketPlace. Following the traditions of Indian garment design, no elastic was allowed; instead, pants had to incorporate drawstrings. No Velcro or zippers could be used. No shorts were allowed and skirts had to be thirty-six inches or longer. Jackets could be exported but they needed to have ties like a traditional jacket design from Kashmir. Fabric had to be 100 percent cotton and a certain amount of handwork needed to be included. The regulations did not challenge MarketPlace as they had already learned that their customers liked the ties on the jackets and preferred the loose and comfortable garments. At one point, MarketPlace decided to try elastic in the pants and go through the quota system, but their customers urged them to "please go back to the drawstrings."

Pushpika personally cleared the first twenty shipments through customs upon their arrival in Chicago. She would fill out all the forms and a custom official would eventually telephone to tell her whether a shipment had passed or not. On the India side, the shipment had to be certified by a government office, the All India Handicrafts Board. A Mumbai officer would come to SHARE and check the shipment before placing a seal on the box. Again, there was potential for corruption. Pushpika recalls that when the first shipment was to leave India,

> The women had everything ready and packed up. But the Handicrafts Board said, "Oh, we can't come for three weeks." It was June or July and the merchandise was needed for the home parties in the fall. Because it was to be shipped by sea, the products would have arrived too late if they did not ship right away. So the official agreed to come "after work." Our antennae went up. We picked him at the train station. The person who was in charge of seeing to the paperwork was a leprosy patient which surprised the official. We served him samosas and tea. We were chatting and he asked questions about the work. He took out and inspected almost everything. My mother was calling that my daughter needed to be fed as I was breast feeding her at the time, but I knew that if I left the officer would have asked the male who was present for a bribe. The officer would not have the courage to ask a woman. They all ended up being there until 9:30 at night and once the officer realized the women were not going home he gave approval and left. We never had any serious problems with certification from that point forward.

As the catalog was developed, garment designs became more sophisticated, with the concept of a line of related garments being introduced. In the mid-1980s, Pushpika had been introduced to a highly creative designer named Kirit Dave who was working in one of the slums with women doing cross-stitch. Pushpika and Kirit found that they got along well because of their mutual interest in building the capacity of the women with whom they were working. Kirit worked with SHARE on and off between 1988 and 1999. He had the ability to be creative and solve problems, and to make the work simple enough for the women to complete. Kirit remained involved with MarketPlace for a number of years, helping to design the line in a production-friendly way.

Organizational Structure

By the time that the first catalog was sent out in fall 1990, over 100 women were working in SHARE. Women gathered in one workshop, where the fabric cutting, machine sewing of garments, quality control, and packing were completed. In a small room in the back, supervisors made up embroidery kits that were distributed for women to complete in their homes. The workshop was located on the edge of the Golibar slum, near where the majority of the artisans lived. Pushpika describes the area as "a shantytown in Santa Cruz East [that is] high density, poor quality (mostly illegal) housing, open sewers, narrow lanes, pollution, and a paucity of many services, such as garbage collection and toilets. Water is either too scarce—as in access to drinking water—or too plentiful, as in the monsoon floods. People there make money any way they can: there are potters, tanners, barbers, rag pickers, maids, bidi rollers, and rickshaw drivers. Some people find employment in the sweatshops located there. These are the living conditions for over half of the population of Mumbai."

The centralized workshops served many important functions during MarketPlace's early years. Functions included developing systems for production planning, working with cash flow, establishing standards for product quality, and establishing practices needed for timely delivery.

Fatima Merchant, a social worker from Mumbai, had joined SHARE as production manager in 1991 when sales had risen to $250,000. While she had no production background, Fatima was very sensitive to the personal and household needs of the women and worked closely with them to understand their personal situations. By the mid-1990s, SHARE expanded to 175 women. Pushpika had two young children by then, so she divided her time between the United States and India. One day while in India, Pushpika asked the women about SHARE and no one knew the name of the organization for which they were working. There was no feeling of ownership that the organization was theirs. As well, as the organization had grown, Fatima had observed that the women needed more opportunities for leadership development. An organization top-heavy with supervisors had lost sight of the mission of assisting artisans at grassroots levels with skill and leadership development in the vertically integrated firm. Fatima suggested that for greater empowerment they might consider separating SHARE into smaller independent artisan groups from which MarketPlace would source their products. MarketPlace already sourced products from two other nonprofit groups besides SHARE, so an example existed.

When Fatima, now executive director of SHARE, and Pushpika approached the women with the idea of decentralizing SHARE into smaller groups, the women did not favor the change. The women were fearful that decentralization would require more responsibility from everyone and they did not feel they had adequate knowledge about how the whole business worked. Two male supervisors for SHARE were the first to volunteer that they wanted to form groups. Then a group of women stepped forward to form a women-only group. Several women who were supervisors at SHARE thought decentralization would not work and left the organization as a result. The transition toward decentralization was difficult and the emerging groups collaborated to ensure that necessary training was provided. Fatima worked closely with the women's group to facilitate its development. Pushpika shared the process with her customers, writing in the catalog that "the year 1995 was a year of many choices and changes for the artisans at SHARE. Two employees have initiated the development of two small cooperatives: Ghar Udyog (meaning home-based enterprise), and WARE (Women Artisans Rehabilitation Enterprise). In addition, forty-five of the SHARE artisans have formed their own cooperative, Udan Mandal (Udan meaning soaring high). SHARE will continue to work with them in an advisory role, guiding and supporting them in developing production planning and financial systems, but the women have total control and responsibility."

The MarketPlace Groups

In retrospect, decentralization was successful, although there were plenty of uncertainties at the time. By the early 2000s, seven groups had formed to produce the MarketPlace products. The groups were now on their own as separate enterprises. From the time of decentralization, MarketPlace emphasized to the artisan groups that they should not become totally dependent on MarketPlace orders and should seek out other firms for which they could produce products. As each new group formed, it was paired with an existing group as a subcontractor for close supervision and guidance. After six months in the mentoring relationship, a group was launched on its own to be responsible for the full range of business activities. Pushpika describes the small indications of emerging ownership that evolved among one of the new fledgling groups.

> When I went to the workshop to see what had been done, I saw that they had put up a small altar where they had pictures of different Gods and a light there. That's very important in Indian culture. Every home will have a small altar. And I felt very good that here this was part of showing their ownership that they had decided we want to have this altar because it's like our house and they are going to represent the different religions.

As part of the reorganization, SHARE continued as an umbrella organization providing social work services to women and children. MarketPlace Bombay, the Mumbai-based commercial structure for the organization, worked with the Chicago office on the business activities. The women interviewed for this book were each members of one of the following seven groups. The following brief descriptions highlight the varying circumstances under which groups were formed and the differing organizational structures that evolved. Two models typify the groups. In one model, groups are financed and led by single individuals, and in the other, groups are organized around a more cooperative structure. The latter is more common among women-only groups.

Ghar Udyog

Ghar Udyog, which translates as "home-based enterprise," was one of the first groups to decentralize under the leadership of a male tailoring supervisor. Originally from Tamil Nadu and educated only through the fourth standard, the supervisor moved from a farming community to Mumbai in hopes of joining the film industry. Instead, he ended up working in a hotel and in the steel industry before learning about opportunities at SHARE. Despite his modest background, the man is a gentle but very strong leader and has in turn encouraged leadership of others. Before becoming a supervisor, he had been a cutter and handled fabric purchases for SHARE. Based on his past difficulty in finding jobs as a male, he knew how much harder it must be for women to find work. Providing opportunities for the women motivated his initiative to start Ghar Udyog. His male cousin provides a strong second line of leadership for the group.

Both men in Ghar Udyog are very creative and knowledgeable about cutting, sewing, pattern making, and grading. They run MarketPlace Bombay's design workshop where styles for each catalog's line are finalized and interior products are designed. Ghar Udyog prepares all the samples for Market-Place. Both men are Muslim, but their group includes both Hindu and Muslim artisans. By the early 2000s, the cohesive group was composed of forty women (ten who sew and thirty who embroider) and five men, all of whom work well together and are trustful and confident of each other. The leader believes it is valuable to involve men in the group as well as women, reporting that "men can do the heavy work of bringing in the fabric and they can go outside [away from the slum and into the larger community]." While first working out of a 10-by-10-ft rental space, Ghar Udyog has relocated several times and now owns a larger two-story workshop in the Golibar slum. As with the other groups, a location in the slum is advantageous as it is just a short walk from the women's homes. Ghar Udyog is able to

produce around 500 garments monthly and tackles any style that Market-
Place orders. The financial success coupled with strong leadership provided
by the second line leader has allowed the originator to pursue a second
business providing block-printed and batik-dyed fabrics for MarketPlace
(see Chapter 5).

WARE

The group WARE (Women Artisans Rehabilitation Enterprise) was started
by another male supervisor who stepped up to the responsibility when
it was offered. The man, educated through the tenth standard, exhibited
entrepreneurial talents in his previous work with paper printing and fast
food delivery, and had supervised tailoring at SHARE. The leader of WARE
does not himself cut, sew, or embroider; rather, his strengths are adminis-
trative and he has handled purchase orders, maintained records, and carried
out production planning for SHARE. Because of his more limited experience with the product, he found it more difficult to build support for
the group. He employed an embroidery supervisor who was very strong
and worked hard on his interpersonal skills with the women. As a result,
many women wanted to work with WARE and by the early 2000s the total
group included forty-eight women and four men. The leader is Christian and
many of the artisans in WARE practice the religion as well. The leader shares
that "Everyone is equal and everyone is treated as equal. I sit and eat with
them. They don't feel scared to tell me problems." WARE started in a small
10-by-10-ft space in the leader's home before moving to a small rented
space. Now the group owns a much larger workshop, which is well-stocked
with shelving, a cutting table, and a computer table. Like the other groups,
the workshop is situated in the slum, within a close walk to the women's
homes. WARE has the capacity to produce 700 to 800 garments a month
of varied difficulty. Like Ghar Udyog, WARE has been successful and
the leader hopes to expand into production of school uniforms for the
local market.

Udan Mandal

Udan Mandal ("soaring high") was started by three women who had worked
in cutting, accounting/management, and tailoring for the early, centralized
SHARE. The three women, two originally from Gujarat and the third from
Mumbai, completed varied levels of formal education, none higher than
the tenth standard. Two are Muslim and the third is Hindu. Two of the
women's work experience before coming to SHARE had been limited to

nursery schools; the third had not been allowed by her family to go out of her house, but did sewing work at home for a neighbor. In contrast to the male leaders of Ghar Udyog and Ware, the three women did not have similar leadership experience. While forty-five women from SHARE initially joined Udan Mandal, many became scared that the organization would not succeed and left to join the two more established groups, leaving Udan Mandal with only eight in the group for awhile. As one of the leaders recalled, "I couldn't handle it all, couldn't do it all, didn't know how to pay proper attention to things." The all-female group faced further difficulties because when formed they had no central place for a workshop. Cutting was done in one leader's home in Bandra and because it was quite a distance from the artisans' homes in the Golibar slum, the stressful travel situation contributed to several women's decisions to leave.

Fatima Merchant worked closely with the Udan Mandal leaders through these difficult periods as they learned how to manage on their own, solve problems, and improve their production skills. Eventually, they were able to rent a space and then buy an even larger workshop in the slum. While the group still required close guidance, by the early 2000s it included a total of twenty-eight women, with sixteen working in embroidery, eight in tailoring, and two supervising; the group could produce around 500 garments a month. Citing the benefits of an all-female group, one leader explained that "We feel a freedom because men are not here. We can share whatever we feel. [The women] have learned to live and deal with the bundles and don't need men."

Pushpanjali

Pushpanjali, "an offering of flowers," was formed in early 1997 by a woman who was originally from a village near Goa but had moved to Mumbai at the age of fifteen because of the need to support her family after her father died. Having an education through the seventh standard, the woman first worked in a garment factory before working as a tailor out of her home. At SHARE, she had worked as a cutter and managed the stock room, but augmented her income during the evenings by teaching women in her slum to embroider. When she started Pushpanjali, she used a room in her house, but now owns a space that was added on above a nursery. While the leader lives over an hour away from the workshop, most of the women are within a ten-minute walk of the workspace. The group started with just eleven women, but slowly added others for a total of thirty-eight women—eleven tailors, twenty-five embroiderers, and two supervisors—who produce between 400 and 500 garments per month. While one of the leader's sons handles the group's accounting, the group members think of themselves as an "all-female" group since "the boy" has been with them from the start, practically growing up as a son with all of them.

A self-described activist, the politically involved leader is very strong on the rights of women. In the slum where the group is located, women tend to be submissive and defer to their husbands. Yet, a majority of the group has faced problems of abuse from alcoholic husbands. The leader scolds them not to sit by, but instead to try and solve their problems, and to stay united as a group. When one woman was being beaten by her husband, the women took her to the police to file a report and the situation has improved. They have also participated in marches against local merchants who treat them poorly or sell them spoiled food.

Ashiana

Ashiana evolved from an enterprise that SHARE had worked with prior to decentralizing. The organization had been started in 1992 by a Scottish nonprofit that ultimately did not maintain much contact with the women over the ensuing years. In 2000, the women discovered that their male supervisor had walked off with a lot of the group's money. When asked to leave, he stole their sewing machine as well. The women regrouped into Ashiana, which stands for "home." Now Ashiana is cooperatively organized and managed by a woman who grew up in Mumbai and is educated through the sixth standard. The group has faced many ups and downs. Not surprising given the group's history, Ashiana has emphasized financial training and skill development for "speaking up." Ashiana's work was made more difficult because at first they did not have a communal space for their work, which meant they were unable to properly secure fabric, take and place orders, and meet and talk for group bonding. Now Ashiana rents a workshop in the slum, just a few minutes' walk from the women's homes. The group is fairly heterogeneous and the eighteen women involved (six tailors, nine embroiderers, and three supervisors) reside in a Mumbai Central slum, an area known for its volatile clashes between Hindus and Muslims. A supervisor wishes that the workshop could be "in a place that is able to inspire these women to get out of the slums." Despite their religious heterogeneity and struggles, the women have a very strong desire to make the organization work, no matter how hard it might be. In efforts to improve, they worked with Ghar Udyog as a subcontractor where two of the women also learned cutting. Now the women are able to produce between 300 and 400 garments a month.

Arpan

Arpan ("an offering") also started with an NGO, but its separation in 1999 was not as divisive as experienced by Ashiana. The twenty-four women who made up the cooperative in the early 2000s are from a community in Thane with a high rate of alcoholism. Arpan rotates the leadership every two to three years, pairing an experienced leader with each new leader. The women are open as a group, speak their opinions, and are eager to learn the skills required for production planning. Due to the women's intense desire to learn, attendance at any training session is good and opportunities are pursued with enthusiasm. Cross training among members ensures there is always someone able to do the necessary work.

Sahara

Sahara was started in 1998 by the younger brother of the leader of Ghar Udyog after he had worked with that group for four years. Originally from Tamil Nadu, the young man was educated through the ninth standard and is adept at problem solving. He had learned tailoring before leaving his village, and was put in charge of materials procurement for Ghar Udyog, as well as supervising cutting. The leader has a strong understanding of quality. Being a little competitive, he brought to his group several of the women who worked for Ghar Udyog and others who worked for Ware. In the early 2000s, Sahara included thirty-two artisans, twenty-nine of whom are women who work as tailors (seven), embroiderers (twenty), and supervisors (two). Sahara owns its two-room workshop, having had to split the group between two rental workshops in the past. The group is able to produce around 1,500 garments per month. Describing his system for providing incentives, the young leader explained, "I bring the group together and point out the women with the highest payments. I tell them their work is appreciated—they appreciate being appreciated and praised." Because of the quality of their work and productivity, the group has been successful in earning large orders from MarketPlace. As well, the group has a few clients in the local market and hopes to attract more in the future.

SHARE and MarketPlace in the Twenty-first Century

As the years have passed, Share and MarketPlace have weathered considerable change. The business activities in producing a catalog and the products for sale have matured. Sales have increased dramatically since the first catalog was produced in 1990. The catalog was expanded from twenty-four to thirty-two pages in 1994 and by 1997, sales topped $1 million. Sales have remained static at this level through 2009. New groups formed as part of decentralization have challenged the artisans in new ways and fostered the women's leadership and social development. Yet, MarketPlace retains characteristics that are at the core of their organizational model. These characteristics describe a fair trade model with a dual focus on the economic and social needs of small producer groups and their artisan members.

With business leveling off in the 2000s, Pushpika looked for strategies to maintain production for the groups in India. While the organization was becoming increasingly sophisticated in optimizing its customer mailing lists for catalog mailings, web sales accounted for 35 percent of total sales while catalog sales were beginning to decline. Pushpika believes that with the larger thirty-six- to thirty-eight-page catalogs they had been producing since the early 2000s, they may have lost their "style," thus leading her to consider reducing the size of the catalog and referring customers to the Web to access the total produce line.

Design and Product Development

While early customers often purchased products primarily because of the MarketPlace mission, an increasingly sophisticated design and product development process has contributed to a MarketPlace signature look that has broader aesthetic appeal. Partly as a result of a season when they ended up with excess fabric, Pushpika, Kirit, and some of the others in Mumbai worked together over a three-week period to develop ways to use the excess by overdyeing the fabric and creating new styles. The group initiative led to the idea of holding a design workshop two times per year in Mumbai in order to develop products for each catalog.

In advance of a workshop, the colors for the next season's line are planned. Then the leader from Ghar Udyog that started the fabric printing business (see Chapter 5) prints 100 or more swatches using an old block for color tests. Meanwhile, Pushpika's artist sister in Chicago, Indira, designs the new blocks, which are then carved in rural India and may take up to two or three months for completion. The fabric printers next complete a second round of swatches using the new blocks. In Chicago, Marketplace initiates the designs of new garments drawing on their customers' input. The designs are then sent to Ghar Udyog, where the first pattern and a sample in leftover fabric or muslin are prepared in anticipation for Pushpika's arrival in India, where she is joined by Kirit or a US designer for that season's lines. In the past four years, a single US designer has been employed as a way to maintain focus on the US customer and her changing needs and to couple that customer demand with the women's changing embroidery skills.

The design workshop involves fourteen to fifteen women with design potential who are also good at embroidery. The two leaders from Ghar Udyog facilitate the workshop. On the first day, all fifty to fifty-five garments are laid out to visualize how they look together. Then the designers get to work with the women embroiderers to plan the embellishment. Women enjoy being part of the workshop and there is some rotation of who is involved. While the women will often step in and say, "Let's try this," they must also be comfortable with the fact that their idea will not always work. Every two to three days, a leader from Ghar Udyog, the designer, and Pushpika review the developing garments to identify which garments may be too expensive for the market or which have too little embroidery. Limited embroidery imparts consequences for reduced earnings among the embroiderers during a season's line. Sometimes embroidery is sized up or down accordingly.

Workshop leaders also visualize which garments will coordinate together as ensembles, check that the embroidery will match, and consider how well the garments will photograph in the catalog. During the review, garments are divided into casual, professional, and more progressive looks. Having the spin-off, fabric-printing shop from Ghar Udyog located nearby to Mumbai has allowed expanded innovation by shortening the time it takes to find out whether a new printing technique works or not. During the design workshop, while Pushpika, the designer, and Ghar Udyog leaders focus on the apparel, the women artisans are almost completely in charge of design for the interior products, an opportunity that helps them expand their understanding about the design process.

Pushpika returns to Chicago following the three-week workshop, after which Ghar Udyog duplicates three sets of samples, two to be sent to Chicago and one to be kept at MarketPlace Bombay. When the samples arrive in Chicago, MarketPlace customers are brought in to rate the line. Meanwhile in Mumbai, specification sheets and patterns are made up along with a sample kit for each garment. The pay scale for a garment is worked out among the groups following time motion studies and using guidelines about hours involved for sewing and embroidery, overhead, and other factors (see Chapter 6 for greater detail on pricing). Ghar Udyog completes the grading of all patterns. Quality representatives from each group come to the office and discuss what could go wrong during production, as they are the ones who will need to oversee quality.

In the mid-2000s, because of financial constraints, MarketPlace began running the two design workshops together and developed slightly smaller lines. They are also rerunning more styles from previous catalogs, thus not reinventing 100 percent of each line. Pushpika, however, does not believe this is good for long-term sales because they need to be more closely in touch with changing apparel trends and offer fresh ideas for customers. Thus, by the mid-2000s, the organization was beginning to consider expanded fabric sourcing and inclusion of a broader range of fabrications, such as knits, or fiber content beyond cotton, such as silk, in order to spur growth.

Production

Based on market research in Chicago, designs are finalized for the line. Pushpika's sister, Lalita, then makes recommendations as to which artisan groups in India should produce the various garments for MarketPlace. The final decisions are made by the group leaders themselves and take into consideration each group's confidence in their ability to produce the style. Production of garments is completed by the seven groups described above and one additional producer group in Gujarat. There are five fabric producers, each specializing in a certain technique. Batik block printing done by UKK (Udog Kala Kendra), the spin-off from Ghar Udyog, comprises 40 to 50 percent of the fabric ordered.

As fabric is ordered by the groups and arrives at MarketPlace Bombay, office staff inspects it for defects. For the first order, it may take up to eight weeks to receive the printed fabric. Production samples are made by each group and the leader of Sahara inspects those for quality, match to measurement specifications, and placement of the fabric patterns and embroidery. There is fairly quick turnaround with production in the early stages of ordering, but it becomes more complicated as follow-up orders are placed. MarketPlace typically orders four times for each season, based first on customer input on the line, then on sales at wholesale markets, next on how the product is placed in the catalog, and finally on actual sales. The first two orders are usually shipped by sea, arriving after forty-five days, while the additional two orders ship by air and arrive in Chicago in around two days.

The producer groups are seldom able to meet the dates they are asked to deliver the goods to MarketPlace Bombay. Major delays tend to occur at the fabric production stage. Water is scarce before the monsoons, so fabric printers must order a tanker of water. In contrast, when the monsoons arrive, the fabric does not dry. As well, color specifications may not be met. The cost of rejected fabric is borne by the fabric producer. Many of the group leaders that we interviewed discussed the difficulty of needing to "chase the fabric" which, when delayed, leaves little time for the garments to be sewn and embroidered. Weekly updates on production status are made by the fabric producers and sewing/embroidery groups. While communication between Mumbai and Chicago has improved considerably, Pushpika recalls the cultural challenges for communicating with the fabric producers in the early years.

> My biggest problem with them is to get them to tell us when they're having problems, like write us a letter. One man turned to me and said, "That's fine, but we only write and receive letters when someone dies and we don't want you to be upset when you get this letter." So, it's a totally different concept for them to write letters. Here I was all worked up and saying, "at least write a letter" but without any clue as to why they weren't. So I went back and promised not to think that someone died if they would just write. Communication is so difficult not just physically but when they are not in the habit of giving bad news.

The departure of SHARE's executive director, Fatima Merchant, in 2005 led to additional production challenges, primarily because a few groups tried taking shortcuts instead of following established procedures for production. The artisan groups producing for the fair trade organization have begun to face the problems typically associated with the mainstream apparel industry, including problems that result in inadequate lead time for production, and several weeks of downtime with no work between seasons.

Beyond Economics: Projects for Skill Building and Leadership

When SHARE was founded, economic empowerment versus charity was of utmost importance. Shortly after that, as the business developed, the organization began to focus on leadership development. With decentralization of production, additional opportunities for leadership were created—each group needed at least one person in charge. As well, two or three women from each group were trained for quality control, not only for inspection of their own group's products but also to join with those from the other groups for checking quality of the entire production lot before it is shipped to Chicago. The design workshops offered yet additional opportunities for leadership.

Pushpika recalls one period when the organization broke its rules about charity and that was with regard to education of children. The time was around 1994 and the women were talking about dreams and aspirations for their lives. The women shared a pivotal vision for educating their children. All the women valued education and were ready to make sacrifices for their children's schooling. As is common in the Indian culture, the women gave first preference to their son's education; however, they wanted to send their daughters to school as well. Even though a large portion of education expenditures is paid by the Indian government, the added expense of providing for uniforms and school supplies was difficult for the women to meet. So MarketPlace decided to initiate a children's education program and encouraged US customers to donate by sponsoring a child. MarketPlace viewed the sponsorship less as charity, but instead as a partnership between the mother and the customer giving the money. Along with the customer's donation, the parents were required to pay a certain amount for each child. In turn, the children had to pass their exams, thus demonstrating they were studying. Furthermore, the preference for which child to educate had to go to the daughter. The child sponsorships program ran for about two and one-half years until MarketPlace saw there was no longer the urgent financial need. MarketPlace then converted the program to the Armaan ("desire") Club, which aimed to provide children with out-of-school enrichment in sports, art, communications, and others (see Chapter 5 for more detail on Armaan Club).

Additional efforts of SHARE and MarketPlace have centered on building skills, improving self-confidence, and educating the women about a wide range of social issues. This work has assisted the women directly and also provided additional leadership opportunities. In the mid-1990s, SHARE, now able to focus on social programs since production had been decentralized, initiated programs with a local NGO on gender sensitivity, women's law, and women's health. Gender sensitivity included training to help the women understand the problems stemming from infanticide, feticide, and under- and malnutrition that result from girls being given only the leftovers that boys do not eat. The women's health topic was important since some of the women were aging and they needed to learn how to take better care of themselves.

Next, a social action program was developed. Pushpika began by holding a conversation with the women about how they could impart a greater impact in their communities. SHARE and MarketPlace had grown beyond their wildest dreams, but Pushpika also knew that even if it grew to 100,000 women, the organizations still addressed only a tiny portion of the human need in India—how could the organizations have even greater impact? The idea came about that each group would choose something in the community that proved problematic and, by taking social action and solving it, the neighborhood would benefit. The groups pursued a variety of social action projects over the years that followed. Some focused on literacy so that the women could understand whether they were being paid properly, others on preventive medicine, and yet others on pollution within the slums. Still another group decided to learn yoga. The choice of yoga initially surprised

Pushpika, but the women explained that as they were going through a stage of their lives of becoming older women, they were facing a lot of tensions at home. They wanted to learn yoga for their health and then teach others. As well, communication with children became more important as the children became teenagers and had to face the temptations and difficulties found in the slums. The social action programs provided additional opportunities for women's leadership.

In addition, when the Global Dialogue program was launched in the catalog as a way of connecting the US customers with the artisans, leaders were assigned from each group to facilitate discussion about selecting topics, writing letters, and taking photographs for the catalog. Some of these new leaders for Global Dialogue had not taken leadership in the social actions projects and they first had to learn to talk in the meetings they held. Pushpika describes strategies such as "the Chairperson Game," used to enhance the women's confidence.

> The women were supposed to think that they were chairpersons for a certain function and while introducing themselves had to speak in third person. The women mentioned that this was the first time that they were exclusively asked about themselves and the whole concept of introducing themselves as a Chairperson in front of others was a exciting experience. The women felt that in their day-to-day life activities hardly did they get an opportunity to speak about themselves, about their liking, their hobbies, and their skills. Most of the women felt that when asked about themselves they could think in terms of their children, their husbands and their family. However, when given a chance it was difficult for them to think exclusively about themselves. But they were asked to think about their hobbies, their skills and one hidden quality. It was really difficult for the women to do this but once they came up to introduce themselves the group helped them to speak. So in this manner the woman explored about herself in a new way and it also helped us in achieving the objective of the exercise.

Although much of the work of SHARE and MarketPlace has focused on women, a small number of men have been involved in the organization since its inception. When the men approached Fatima Merchant and asked for their own group, it became clear that they wanted social development as well. The men shared that they were facing a number of issues including a growing disconnect between their relationships with women in the workplace and with their wives. When they come to work, the men understood that women had rights and privileges and they needed to involve the women in decision making. However, when they went home, they were expected to be the head of the family and make all the decisions. Spousal abuse sometimes erupted.

The CACTUS group (Care and Concern Toward Us) was started to serve the men; however, at the time there were only a few men involved in SHARE. They experimented with inviting the husbands of the women to be part of the group, but the plan failed miserably. Some husbands came to the first couple of meetings and then stopped coming. The husbands were unaccustomed to the perspective of the men within the SHARE network who thought of women as equals. For example, the leader of WARE explained in an initial meeting how he went home at the end of one day and started sweeping the floor. His wife went nuts, saying, "What are the neighbors going to think?" The artisans' husbands were not interested in changing their lives in these sorts of ways. Moving forward in time, the CACTUS group is now composed of men and women, the latter involving the female supervisors and group leaders. The men invited the women as they want a woman's perspective on issues under discussion. For example, they are learning about AIDS and will communicate what they learn back with their groups and neighborhoods. The men also wanted to learn how to better communicate and work with women in similar management positions as their own. One CACTUS member shares his perspective.

> I have learned about gender bias and how patriarchal Indian society is. Exposure to all these new ideas has brought about a lot of change in my thinking and my attitude. But it is not all that easy to implement these thoughts, as you don't get support and encouragement from your relatives and from society. But one thing I can say now is that I have a better understanding of both my wife and all the women artisans working with me.

The Evolution of MarketPlace

From its inception, income generation and social development shared center stage of the MarketPlace fair trade model. Pushpika Freitas drew on her experiences growing up with a mother who spearheaded social work in Mumbai, and on her own academic training as she applied social work's holistic framework for human development. Over time, MarketPlace artisans acquired a skill set that served both for business growth and for enactment in their personal lives. Attention to the artisans' health, their children's education, and their household traumas never served as side or secondary issues, but were addressed in tandem with the acquisition of apparel production skills. The artisans' voices always played a major role in organizational decision making.

As the artisans' skills and interpersonal skills developed, they were offered new production and leadership opportunities. Over time, the women's frame of reference expanded from their households and the workshops to encompass efforts toward improving health and well-being in their communities. Pushpika sums up the impacts of their MarketPlace work.

> What really excites me about MarketPlace is that it does not impose solutions to problems. Rather, it gives opportunities to people to take control of their lives, to find happiness and to make a difference in society by creating their own solutions to social and cultural problems.

CHAPTER 4

Daily Life as a MarketPlace Artisan

My husband sent me away soon after my marriage because I could not give the dowry he hoped for. He beat me badly during the few months we were married. I returned to my parent's house but I was a burden, and they urged me to look for a job to help the household.

My husband was making furniture. His money was not enough. Also, he had TB. I had to manage the two children. Then I got TB for ten months. So we owed much to hospitals. I needed to find work.

I am educated in the Hindi medium and it was of no use. I wanted to send my children to English medium school, but my husband's income was not enough. Then some of the women saw my work and told me to go to MarketPlace.

Family crises, health challenges, and an aspiration to educate young children act as catalysts in attracting women to MarketPlace. In this chapter, we initiate their journey as MarketPlace artisans by describing their daily routines and the life experiences they bring to their work. The overview is intended to introduce the artisans as we met them in May 2001 and to offer a perspective on the cultural context of their lives. The background forms a base from which to assess our interviews conducted across a twenty-one-month period, ending in January 2003.

We begin the chapter by first traveling to the Mumbai slums, where artisans reside and workshops are located.[1] Through photographs of daily routines, artisans provide insight on how they integrate household responsibilities and MarketPlace work in their daily lives. We then offer an individual and familial portrait of the artisans who participated in our research. The chapter ends with a review of critical life circumstances that brought the artisans to MarketPlace.

Daily Life in the Slums of Mumbai: Cameras Tell the Story

Collecting water, scrubbing floors, caring for children, and cooking dominate women's lives in the Golibar, Thane, and Central Bombay slums of Mumbai. MarketPlace sewing and embroidery further contribute to a multifaceted daily routine. In order to more clearly understand how women integrate their household responsibilities with textile production, we asked twenty-six women who reside in the Golibar slum to record their days using cameras.[2] Our directions stated,

> We want you to include pictures of your activities during the day, from when you arise in the morning until going to bed. These can be of anything as long as they tell something about who you are, your work, your family, and the neighborhood where you live.

Supplied with cameras, the women enthusiastically set off to photodocument their homes, families, and daily life. Once the film was processed, we asked the women to select from the twenty-four photos a series that depicted a typical day. These photos then formed the basis for discussing "who you are and about your life."[3] As they talked, women described their average of nearly seventeen waking hours as composed of three sets of activities: household tasks other than cooking, cooking, and MarketPlace work (see Figure 4.1).

Figure 4.1 Hours devoted to daily activities.

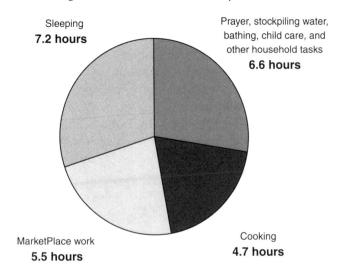

Sleeping
7.2 hours

Prayer, stockpiling water, bathing, child care, and other household tasks
6.6 hours

MarketPlace work
5.5 hours

Cooking
4.7 hours

Household Tasks

Early morning, between 4:00 and 6:00 a.m., women begin the day in prayer. Hindu women perform the morning *puja* at a flower-decorated platform altar attached to a wall of their 10-by-10-ft single-room homes. A small statue of the primary household deity provides focus to the prayers. As one artisan explains, "It is important to remember God every day, even if only for a few minutes. Then you feel good in the heart." Stockpiling the family's daily water supply and bathing follow next in order. Gathering water from a neighborhood tap occupies an average of forty minutes, but ranges from as little as thirty minutes up to two hours for certain women (see Figure 4.2). In some cases water is carried by hand and in others siphoned with a hose through a window to a holding tank in the living quarters. Because water

Figure 4.2 Gathering water.

is available in each neighborhood of the slum for only a few hours each morning, women's daily regimen exhibits little latitude during those hours when water is available. Women must be at home during the early morning hours to collect this essential household commodity. As one woman explains, "Without water, we cannot do anything—make tea, cook, or bathe."

Across the average of seven hours devoted to household tasks, women focus exclusively on their families and, in addition to gathering water, thoroughly scrub the cement floors each day. As one woman assesses, "I have to scrub the floors every day, even if I am sick. No one else will do it." Mothers also direct attention to their children as they lather and bathe them, dress them in immaculate school uniforms, and carefully braid daughters' hair (see Figures 4.3 and 4.4). As she brushed her daughter's hair in the early morning, a mother reflects,

> Getting my daughter ready for school is important because my daughter's schooling will change her life and allow her not to have to face the same life I have faced.

Because families often cannot afford rickshaw or bus transportation for their children, mothers, with young daughters and sons in tow, walk them to and from school across roads clogged with traffic.

Figure 4.3 Scrubbing the floor.

Figure 4.4 Bathing the baby.

Cooking

Particularly salient are the average of 4.7 hours per day spent in food-related activities (see Figures 4.5 and 4.6), including shopping for ingredients in nearby markets, cutting vegetables and grinding spices, forming and heating chapattis, stirring curry sauces, serving and eating meals, and washing dishes. Much of food preparation is conducted while sitting on the floor, with women on hands and knees bending over to cut vegetables, grind spices, and roll out numerous portions of roti. Meal times foster physical closeness and numerous intergenerational contacts among families as they sit together at midday and evening meals. Artisans point to the importance of cooking for their families.

> It is very important to eat. If we don't we could fall sick. So, even if we have little, we eat because health is important to maintain.

> As a housewife, I need to help my husband be strong. And to eat is to do this. He was once very sick with [tuberculosis] and very thin. As you can see now, that is not the case.

MarketPlace Work

After completion of household cooking responsibilities, women feel free to walk the short distance to their nearby MarketPlace workshops to pick

Figure 4.5 Cutting vegetables.

up bundles of fabric for sewing and embroidery. For about half of the women, MarketPlace work commences around 10:00 or 11:00 a.m., but for the remainder with heavier household tasks work begins between 2:00 and 3:00 p.m. Textile work, occupying an average of 5.5 hours, often continues well into the evening (see Figure 4.7). However, throughout the afternoon and evening, artisans intermingle their sewing and embroidery with supervision of children's games and homework (see Figure 4.8) while also stopping to serve and eat the evening meal. Sitting on the floor, women often work under a single low wattage light bulb that is hung from the center of the room and provides the only illumination in the space. Women finish their sewing at 8:00 or 9:00 p.m.; some artisans continue on up to 11:00 p.m. or midnight if completion of a large order is urgent.

Figure 4.6 Stirring curry.

Women talk with pride about their sewing and speak fondly of the social bonds of support they establish with other MarketPlace women from different religions and backgrounds. Women describe the courage they gain to speak their opinions openly and to shelter other women with common problems. For many women, joining MarketPlace becomes a first step outside the

Figure 4.7 Embroidering for MarketPlace.

Figure 4.8 Assisting with homework.

household and toward an independent identity from that of their husbands or in-laws. The women perceive themselves as part of a shared struggle with other women. Not only do the women learn a skill at MarketPlace, but they also pass it on to others. One artisan spoke of the delight she experienced in her daily encounters with other women:

> Several women from Sahara live in my community and we sometimes do our work together. It is fun. We're also teaching a young girl a career so she too can support her family.

Women compare themselves to their neighbors who do not have MarketPlace jobs or who do not appear to use time productively.

> My embroidery shows that I am working on my own feet, that I am not a burden on anyone. If there is a problem, even I can help.

> Bombay is so crowded that there is a lot more people than work so people have to chase the work. My photo shows me making money and having work.

Reflections From Photodocumentation

Artisans' photodocumentation of typical days provides abundant insight about their homes, household tasks, and integration of work with family. As they discuss their residences, women exhibit great pride in their small, immaculate, one-room homes and in the improvements they have made through money earned at MarketPlace. For some artisans, saving money to add a second floor room not only adds space for the family but also contributes to expanded household income when the room can be rented out to others seeking hard-to-find living quarters within the densely packed slum. The acquisition of consumer goods points to laborsaving devices (such as a larger water tank or better cooking utensils) as well as provides some families with entertainment (such as television or music) not available in the past.

As for household tasks, MarketPlace artisans are part of a global gender ideology in which poor women assume major responsibility for mobilizing household resources for survival (Rosenbaum 2000; Wilkinson-Weber 1999). The artisans' photographs place in perspective the average of eleven-plus hours that are spent by Indian women in completing the critical tasks that provide for their family's most basic needs. In particular, Indian food preparation is time-intensive, and without refrigeration, requires daily shopping for essential ingredients.

In watching how women integrate their work and families, a nonlinear pattern emerges to their days. Women alternate back and forth from one activity to another, leaving a limited number of sequential, uninterrupted hours for MarketPlace clothing production. Blocks of time for sewing and embroidery ranged from 1.5 to 6.1 hours, with an average of 4.2 hours without interruptions. MarketPlace, in recognizing this dilemma, offers flexibility to the artisans such that tailoring and embroidery can be interspersed with cooking, childcare, and other tasks.

In addition, as shown in Figure 4.9, women range widely in the hours they devote to their textile work on a daily basis. Women in the high production group (Group #1) average nine hours per day (range = 7.5-10 hours), whereas those in the low production group (Group #3) with heavy household responsibilities commit a little less than two hours a day to their MarketPlace work (range = one-half to three hours).[4] However, even for women in Group #3, with fourteen hours devoted to household tasks and cooking, MarketPlace employment of only a few hours a day offers these women some opportunity to generate income.

In summary, photoelicited discussions of women's typical days highlight and make salient that flexible hours and the opportunity to work at home are essential to women who are often solely responsible for managing their households across an average of eleven hours interspersed throughout a day. Without additional household help or affordable childcare, these women are simply not free to leave their homes for the long periods of time that would be demanded by other forms of employment, such as domestic labor as a maid or cook or when working at a factory. In contrast, the option to walk

Figure 4.9 Percentage of time for daily activities.

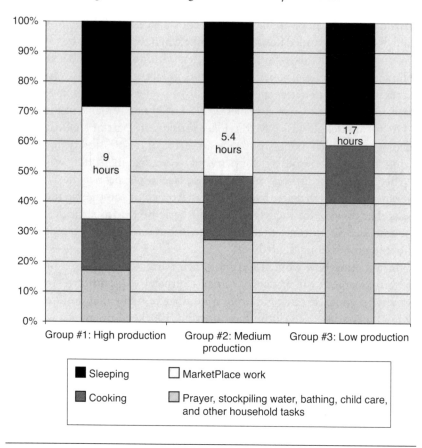

a short distance to a MarketPlace workshop, pick up the allotted supplies, and return to sew at home in the midafternoon and evening appears to be one of few income generation alternatives open to many of the artisans. MarketPlace's textile production strategy clearly matches the cultural context for the lives of many women in Mumbai slums.

MarketPlace Artisans and Their Families

To more fully describe the cultural context of the 161 MarketPlace artisans we interviewed, we offer a demographic portrait of the artisans and their families. The sketch is intended as additional background for assessing the impacts of artisan work at MarketPlace in Chapters 5 through 7. To initiate

Table 4.1 Age, education, and schooling of MarketPlace artisans

CHARACTERISTIC	PERCENTAGE
Age	
Under 20	3.4
20-29	30.4
30-39	45.9
40-49	19.6
50 and over	0.7
Age at marriage	
10-14	20.2
15-19	56.5
20-24	19.4
25-30	3.9
Years of schooling	
No schooling	15.7
1-5	19.5
6-9	47.2
10	13.8
11-14	3.8
Years of employment with MarketPlace	
2 years or less	28.2
3-6	35.9
7-10	28.2
Over 10 years	7.7

the portrait, artisans ranged broadly in age from the youngest at eighteen years old to the oldest at age fifty-five, who was considered "very old" by the other women. However, with an average age of thirty-three years, the majority are in their twenties and thirties (see Table 4.1). Three-quarters are currently married, while another 12 percent have been widowed. Although the women are relatively young, many have been married for ten to fifteen years. Ages at marriage range from ten to thirty years, with an average of eighteen years. For over half of the artisans (58 percent), Mumbai is not their "native place"; rather, they migrated to Mumbai to join their husbands at the time of marriage.[5]

In India, primary school encompasses standards 1 through 5; standards 6 through 10 compose secondary school. A significant marker for school achievement involves passing exams at the completion of Standard 10. The exam offers matriculation into senior secondary school or college (standards 11 and 12) with a specific content focus (such as science and math, communications, commerce, or the arts). After Standard 12, students once again sit for exams to vie for highly competitive university entrance. For the MarketPlace artisans, a little over one-third of the artisans bring either no formal schooling (16 percent) or primary school experience (20 percent) to their work at MarketPlace (see Table 4.1). In contrast, just under half have completed some high school, but only 14 percent successfully passed the Standard 10 exam. Only one artisan has a university degree.

The religious orientation of MarketPlace artisans includes 66 percent Hindus, 30 percent Muslims, and 4 percent Christians. Of the seven MarketPlace workshops, two are exclusively Hindu in membership (Arpan and Pushpanjali). One group is closely balanced in religious membership between Muslims and Hindus (Ghar Udyog), whereas the other four have a higher percentage of Muslims (Ashiana) or Hindus (Sahara, Ware, and Udan Mandal). Only one group, Ware, has a sizeable portion of Christian members (13 percent). Within the Mumbai slums, while the artisans may reside next door to each other, they formerly limited their daily exchanges to others of similar religious faith. Accordingly for many women, the Market-Place workshops provide the first opportunity to talk with and work closely among women with varying spiritual beliefs and viewpoints. Commonalities among the women emerge during animated discussions of early marriages, dashed hopes for education, and difficult home lives.

Moving from individual to household characteristics, children, husbands, and joint or extended family members dominate women's lives in the Mumbai slums.[6] Of the 87 percent of artisans who have children, the average number of children is three; overall, boys and girls are equal in number. Only 14 percent of the women have more than four children. While the households of MarketPlace artisans average 5.3 members, they also range from two on up to an extended family of thirteen. Joint households are common. Beyond the nuclear family, other household members may include in-laws, adult siblings, or nieces or nephews who have arrived seeking work in Mumbai.

Slum density, alcoholism, intergeneration family problems, and financial hardships lead to tense and abusive household encounters with husbands and in-laws. While 18 percent of the artisans admit to currently encountering an abusive situation, SHARE (Support the Handicapped's Rehabilitation Effort) social workers report the incidence to be far higher. The social workers report that in several of the groups, over 90 percent of the members regularly experience abuse that is closely associated with alcohol and drugs. Fights escalate when there are slowdowns in MarketPlace production, resulting in reduced income. Abuse ranges from verbal arguments to sexual abuse and beatings.

> He has tried to strangle me, stab me, and there is constant sexual abuse. Every day he tells me I have to fulfill his needs. I refuse and say this is too small a place and my daughters tell me they don't like it.

> When my husband is drunk he hits me. I keep quiet because if I speak out he just hits me more. My mother-in-law tells me to just "let him be" when he is drunk and violent.

Women often enter their marriages with mindsets that abuse is to be expected and passivity the normative response. Women experience conflicting emotions with their in-laws. Submissively accepting the maltreatment is engrained and hard to amend. Two women tell their personal stories with in-laws.

> I had expected the abuse from my in-laws, so I have persevered. I just accepted that it was part of getting married, or at least that was what I was told. I learned to keep it quiet because I did not want the abuse to have an effect on the children. With my husband, it got better once I finally had a child after five years of marriage.

> My in-laws are verbally abusive and are always bugging me. It's not physical, just verbal. I say, "empty vessels make the most noise." I feel the problems stem from the differences in our generations. I have learned to keep my mouth shut because I need to respect older people.

However, some women have bravely voiced their opinions.

> There was a time after my husband died that my mother-in-law asked me to leave the house and leave my children with her. But, as the house was in my name, I told her I would never leave my children. She should be the one to leave.

With cheap alcohol readily available in the slums, alcoholism creates numerous family conflicts. While some women try to hide spousal outbreaks from those living nearby, others shelter their children with neighbors or sit outside with friends until tensions settle. A woman describes,

> Before I joined [name of group] my husband used to beat me. Now he only fights with me about the children and how we spend money on

them. But, when we fight, sometimes the neighbors come out to see what is happening. I want to avoid that. I want to avoid conflict so I keep quiet.

As their children become older and stronger, sons protect their mothers. As women gain strength from their MarketPlace experiences, they transfer their confidence to confronting their husbands.

When my husband was drinking a great deal, I wouldn't let him come into the house for a year. I told him that I was a supervisor and I didn't want him to come to the house. During that time I would put 100 or 200 rupees near the doorstep for him. I didn't want him in the house as other [name of group] artisans were coming to the house and I felt it was a bad example. Now he yells at me some, but I tell him "I am working and do not go out with men."

Another woman with an alcoholic husband describes the direct support she received from her artisan colleagues. After a particularly brutal beating, the women in her workshop took her to the police to file a report of the attack. The police went to her house and told her husband not to touch her again. The group keeps the written report at the workshop office as proof of the incidence. They fear he may tear up the official report and recommence his beatings. Although examples of group support such as this proliferate, the artisan group members are careful not to overstep their bounds, knowing that an intervention could turn a simmering conflict into a more dangerous eruption.

To recap the MarketPlace portrait, a typical artisan is in her early thirties, has been married for ten years, and has three children. Her joint household includes her immediate family along with in-laws or grown siblings. She has completed some secondary schooling and, whether Hindu or Muslim, engages with women of other faiths in carrying out her MarketPlace work. Alcoholism, in-law conflicts, and poverty often contribute to a disquieting household, the site where she embroiders or sews for MarketPlace in the afternoon and evening.

Joining MarketPlace

Previous work experiences and factors motivating women to seek employment with MarketPlace provide yet another point of view on the cultural context surrounding artisans' lives. At the time of the interviews, artisans had worked with MarketPlace for an average of 5.3 years. Yet, a little over one-quarter were relatively new employees of two years or less, while another 8 percent had made a long-term commitment of eleven to twenty-two years (see Table 4.1). In their MarketPlace work, nearly three-quarters (73 percent) of the women focus on embroidery, 23 percent on tailoring, and a small number (3 percent) navigate back and forth between embroidery and tailoring.

Artisans describe a plethora of individual and household problems that drove their search for employment and eventual arrival at MarketPlace. Insufficient household income, family illness, widowhood or abandonment, and the need to support young children highlight the list. For many artisans, a neighbor or family member who was already employed with MarketPlace witnessed the artisan's distress and introduced her to the organization.

The need for additional money to support a household and pay for special household expenses repeatedly surfaces. Households with several daughters face heavy burdens of impending dowry and marriage expenses. While many husbands work (such as by driving an autorickshaw, vending vegetables from a cart, selling paan, or doing carpentry), jobs are often temporary or irregular. Their incomes do not sufficiently cover household expenses. Money is especially critical when husbands become unemployed or a wife is widowed or abandoned by her husband. Several women provide details.

> My husband left me. I had a year-and-a-half-old child at the time and needed work badly. A neighbor introduced me to one of the supervisors at Ghar Udyog. He told me that it would be hard work and it was. At the beginning I would bring the work home and not remember how to do it. Slowly, slowly, I got better at the embroidery.

> I live with my brother and his family. I have one boy and two girls. Because it is a joint family, I have to work. I want to take responsibility for my children and bring them up myself. I do not want to depend on my brother.

> My father is only a carpenter. The dowry is very high in Uttar Pradesh [her native place]. My sisters and I had to start working to bring up the dowry.

While husbands are not always supportive of their wives taking a job outside the home, many gradually adopt a more positive attitude toward the steady income that MarketPlace provides for the household. A wife who initially kept her work secret from her husband tells,

> After eight or ten days my husband discovered that I was working. He was very angry at first. "Why are you working when I am working?" he

wanted to know. I made him understand that now the children were not going hungry and that things were going more smoothly in the house. He became supportive.

Health problems abound in the Mumbai slums where the artisans live. Women told of mental problems, tuberculosis, loss of eyesight, thyroid illness, polio, joint pain, paralysis, heart problems, and high blood pressure. Weakness resulting from tensions, worry, and malnutrition is particularly common. Three artisans describe health problems that directly led to their need for generating income.

> My husband fell sick with problems in his head and severe and constant headaches. He was in a bad state with memory loss for five months but has made some recovery. I had to find work, and I had small children so I needed to work at home. I came daily [to MarketPlace] pleading for work and finally they gave me work.

> My mother-in-law was sick. I needed money and the doctor said I should get a job where I could work at home and watch my mother-in-law. A friend suggested MarketPlace.

> My father died ten years ago and there was no one to look after the house. Then my elder sister got married and my mother was not well mentally. I quit school to look after things.

Women yearn to provide a good education for their children. Many want to earn enough to pay for expensive English medium schooling, which they perceive as far superior to Hindi medium schooling.

> I was sending my children to the English medium school but my husband did not really approve. When I was unable to pay the fees, the school sent a letter saying I must pay or have my children leave the school, so I went looking for work everywhere.

> We stayed in a good flat owned by my in-laws, but my father-in-law had to sell it because of business problems. The children were in English medium school and my in-laws wanted to send them to another school [Hindi medium], but I wanted to keep them there. I couldn't afford the fees so I joined MarketPlace to pay the fees.

All too often, multiple precipitating factors lead women to MarketPlace. Financial problems, evolving from an ill or unemployed husband, escalate as the family goes hungry or the children's schooling is interrupted. The many husbands who drink heavily or use drugs further exacerbate the already-tense households. Several women describe these intercorrelated household problems that drew them to MarketPlace.

> My husband was ill. He was unemployed and often drunk. Some days my children did not have enough money for transport to school. The sewing work that I was doing at home was not enough to feed the children.

> Our financial conditions were not so good. My husband was sick, and we did not have enough money to care for him and to provide for our family. My in-laws had thrown us out because they did not want to pay for his treatment any more. So, after this we lived in the street until we built a bamboo and mat house in an isolated place in Mumbai. My friend was in the MarketPlace group and she invited me to come work there.

Clearly, the great majority of artisans arrive at MarketPlace with urgent need for income to support their families. For a little over half of the artisans (56 percent), MarketPlace represents either a first job or a new job following a period of unemployment. These women are making little or no contribution to household income at the time of their arrival at Marketplace. The remaining artisans enter MarketPlace either from another regular job or from informal sector employment, usually carried out in the home. Among those artisans who held what they described as "regular" jobs, several women held clerical or sales jobs, where a twelve-hour day was common. Others worked in the garment or food industries, or at factories where plastics were manufactured or screen printing took place. One woman had advanced to the position of supervisor in a jeans factory. While several women clearly valued their factory jobs, others felt that they worked long hours with little pay. A screen painter offered, "I used to only get 300 rupees per month and had to work twelve hours per day." Another described,

> Before, I made papas for which I earned fifteen to sixteen rupees a day. I would work for eight hours and sometimes produce as much as nine to ten kilos, for which I was paid three rupees for a kilo. When I was pregnant I found this work to be very hard and often felt faint, but I had to work as we needed the money.

For several women, marriage led to leaving the factory. As one woman explained,

> I used to work at a company to make cassettes. I also worked at a company making some sculptures and also as a sales clerk. I had always

worked at big companies. But when I got married, my husband wanted me to work at Pushpanjali because it was a woman's group. He did not like big companies.

As compared to "regular" jobs, far more women participated in the informal economy, where they earned "very little money" at what were described as "not reliable" and "not proper" jobs. Women with a sewing machine in their homes stitched clothing for their neighbors, made headbands, or finished saris. Other women produced light bulbs, counted pills in bottles for dispensaries, made bindis, and strung beads. One woman explained that she earned six rupees for each twelve strings of beads, or "next to nothing plus a lot of eye strain." In addition to eyestrain, other illnesses occurred, yet some women saw few alternatives to their at-home work.

> I used to go to residences to wash clothes and to clean and wash utensils. I didn't like this as I got sick from working in the water all the time.

> I used to do a little tailoring at home but I wasn't even making twenty-five rupees [per day] at home. But, I couldn't go out to work because I needed at least twenty-five rupees to have someone look after my children and I saw no prospect of earning this.

To summarize, the MarketPlace women residing in Mumbai slums carry out time-intensive and physically demanding daily tasks that are critical to their household's most basic functioning, whether that be carrying water, preparing simple meals, or caring for young children. Many women suffer from illness and face both physical and mental abuse. Yet, they are dependent on their husbands and in-laws and passively accept what others in the household tell them to do. Women have little awareness of the commonality in their lives, even with nearby female neighbors, and do not know how or where to seek help. Income generation opportunities are scarce in the slums. Finding work is exacerbated by the women's lack of employment skills and their rudimentary education. Despite this profusion of challenges, women hold out the hope that the lives of their children can be better than their own and are desperate to find ways for this to happen.

Notes

1. The word "slum" is used by the participants in this research to describe their neighborhoods composed of densely packed one-room homes with few amenities such as in-home water or toilet facilities.

2. The process for the photoelicitation and related data analysis is described in the appendix.

3. Photographs in this chapter were taken by the artisans. Artisans provided permission for their publication.

4. The three groups were formed on the basis of breaks in the natural-forming clusters within the overall range of one-half to ten hours devoted to MarketPlace work.

5. The phrase "native place" is commonly used by the artisans to refer to the community where they grew up and lived prior to marriage. Artisans frequently express the desire to visit their native place, often in a rural area, on a yearly basis; however, the cost of transportation precludes many from making the annual journey.

6. At the time of marriage, a woman moves to the household of her husband. Under the watchful eyes of her mother-in-law, a daughter-in-law performs extensive household duties. Households can be large, as they include any adult unmarried children, as well as wives and children of other married sons.

CHAPTER 5

Capabilities

I try to get my work finished on time so that I will be given more work. It is important to give the work a good finish. I would like to be able to do more. I watch what the others do and this helps me think that I can do more too.

I have gained a lot of knowledge about tailoring. As new people come in I am responsible for telling them what to do and this makes me feel very nice. I used to take knowledge and now I give it.

All the ladies that come to Udan Mandal were scared to talk to others. They depended on their husband or fathers. Since coming, they are able to speak on their own.

Fair trade enterprises place high priority on developing artisans' technical aptitude, management expertise, interpersonal skills, and self-respect. A supportive environment assists women in transformation from passive receivers to active agents of change for their lives. An organizational culture of transparency permeates the firm. The enterprises act upon the assumption that capabilities, acquired under conditions of open sharing, both contribute to increased income and act as vehicles for artisan empowerment in the workplace, at home, and in the community. In Chapter 5 we address this premise by reviewing capabilities that artisans have gained at MarketPlace.[1] We first describe business skills that contribute to enhancing individual and group capacity and to solving of production problems under challenging circumstances. Second, we explore artisans' newfound communication and interpersonal skills, as these play a part in building confidence and courage for decision making beyond the workshop. That children have the opportunity to share in their mothers' skill building has led to a program for children to acquire new capabilities as well. In a third section, we explore the artisans' reactions to membership in all-women versus mixed-gender workshops as it impacts capability acquisition. Finally, several offshoot businesses are described. The businesses present evidence of entrepreneurial application of capabilities acquired as MarketPlace artisans.

Together, the sections in this chapter address the question posed by development practitioners: Are artisan enterprises merely a survival strategy or are they also contributing to asset building?

Business and Technical Skills: Enhancing Production Capacity

Technical production and business skills provide the foundation from which MarketPlace artisans earn their livelihood. Some artisans arrive at MarketPlace with embroidery or sewing skills, whereas others learn these skills from the beginning. For those artisans who are motivated, responsibilities progress quickly. As one woman explains, "I didn't even know how to thread a needle and now I am knowing so much that there is nothing at the workshop I cannot do." Among women with some preexisting skills they had used to sew for their families, "being paid for our work" provides an incentive for achieving higher standards of quality. For all women, working to precise production specifications for placement of embroidery stitches, seam lengths, and garment sizing are new experiences that contribute to their proficiency for competing in the global marketplace.

Meeting specifications for producing multiple garments in a single size can be challenging in the Indian context. For example, tape measures purchased in the local markets can range in length by several centimeters. When used in the workshops, garments can vary by small gradations that are unacceptable for the export market to the United States. Cultural practices add other challenges. One supervisor's question "You mean you want all size ten jackets to be exactly like all other size ten jackets?" conveyed his puzzlement as to how US women of slightly different weights and body contours could all wear the same size. He continued, "Wouldn't each woman want a jacket that fit her perfectly?" His perspective drew upon the Indian cultural practice whereby individuals go to a tailor who sews clothing precisely to fit each client.

When asked to enumerate specific production skills they have learned, artisans offer an extensive list, including neater and cleaner work, more complex designs, greater speed, and new stitches, color combinations, and finishing techniques. Many artisans demonstrate persistence in learning these new skills. One artisan tells of wanting to learn even more.

> My stitching is improving. I have not reached perfection yet. Having to open up and redo the work when I have made a mistake has made me work harder and really learn.

> I am very interested in the embroidery work that we do. Every time that I have some free time I try to do new designs. I am constantly trying to improve my work.

> There once was an order of bags with plastic inside and a zipper. I was very scared but I had to do this job because the others had gone to their native places [rural homes]. The supervisor asked me to try. I made only one bag the first day, but then made three or four each day for the next few days . . . Nothing is impossible at Sahara.

> For now I am proud of my work, but I will be even more proud and satisfied when I am able to have a more creative input, such as a personal design.

In addition to enhancing their sewing skills, artisans acquire a marketing approach to their work as they learn about customer demand from halfway around the world. Artisans recognize that external markets have different aesthetic preferences. They enjoy making garments that at times seem somewhat strange to an Indian eye.

> My neighbors tease me and ask me what kind of clothes I am making. I tell them that I am making clothes for people outside the country. My neighbors ask me why the clothes are so dark. I tell them that people outside the country have light skins; so dark clothes look good on them. I like to tell them these things.

Artisans clearly learn that their personal preferences differ from those of their customers. A group of women sitting in saris of bright orange, yellow, pink, and blue commented on the MarketPlace clothing in darker hues.

> We like them [the jackets] because people in the U.S. buy them and bring us work. They look good in the catalog and on their skin, but they are not the bright colors that we love.

Artisans acknowledge that production slows and their incomes decline when they must take time to learn to make new products for US customers who expect change in product lines across seasons of a year. However, they also find that making the same products over and over becomes boring. They have clearly grasped the marketing concept that without change, overall sales can decline.

While all artisans note improvements in their sewing or embroidery skills, some also take on broader production responsibilities (see Table 5.1).[2] Artisans have gained confidence to participate in quality control and to travel to retail stores in Mumbai to source buttons, thread, and embroidery yarn; smaller percentages participate in cutting, production planning, collecting of fabric at the train station, and delivering orders.

In workshops with a cooperative organizational structure, production responsibilities are spread broadly so that all members eventually gain

Table 5.1 Production responsibilities and new capabilities
of MarketPlace artisans

CHARACTERISTIC	PERCENTAGE
Production responsibility	
Conducting quality control	23.9
Sourcing supplies	23.3
Collecting fabric from the main office	15.7
Delivering orders to the main office	15.7
Cutting fabric	8.8
Maintaining workshop records	5.7
Planning production	5.0
Communication and travel capabilities	
Speaking out in meetings	72.5
Going out from the slum	59.4
Taking on responsibilities	59.4
Using public transportation	58.0
Using the telephone	49.3
Visiting other workshops	37.7
Reading	19.6
Writing	17.4

Note: For both production responsibilities and for communication and travel capabilities, artisans could indicate as many as applied to their situations. Thus the percentages do not add to 100 percent.

experience in selecting notions for sewing, judging quality, or delivering and collecting fabrics. As an example, members of the Arpan workshop take production planning very seriously and participate in cross training of various tasks. Members maintain detailed notebooks of their calculations; the notebooks serve as references for all members. Arpan members are particularly aware of the importance of each group member contributing her part to the production equation. When cooperation doesn't occur, the plan is disrupted. As one member explained,

> Several of the women say that they can't work, as their children are ill, or some other reason. This continues to be a problem. But we need everyone's input to insure that we complete an order based on our plan. The women who travel to Santa Cruz [location of MarketPlace office] for deliveries often have to leave their children home alone. There are no alternatives. We are angry when others won't help.

Arpan members also diligently apply concepts from training sessions offered periodically by outside consultants. To demonstrate the concept of value-added time, Arpan artisans have rearranged their workshop for greater efficiencies (such as storing the cardboard patterns near the cutting table rather than on a wall across the workshop). In addition, they now plan their out-of-workshop trips to encompass multiple tasks rather than leaving the workshop to run separate errands each time a need arises.

The artisans' creativity in problem solving and dedication to their work emerges at times when orders are particularly heavy, the monsoons arrive, or an emergency surfaces. An artisan described a time that she was delivering an order by autorickshaw to the MarketPlace office. Upon arrival, the products were counted. Only then did she realize that she had left several items behind in the rickshaw. Horrified, she and her sons set out to find the items and, despite the thousands of rickshaws in the Golibar area and following hours of searching, miraculously found the rickshaw with the garments still intact.

As artisans become more knowledgeable about production planning, they begin to value the part that their individual work contributes to completing a larger order that the workshop must deliver to the MarketPlace office by a specific date. As deadlines draw near, women who are ill or who have not completed their allotted embroidery give garments to other artisans to complete. While earning less for themselves, the entire order is finished on time for the benefit of the entire workshop group. Workshops that deliver their orders on time stand to receive even larger orders in the future.

As a summary illustration of production capabilities, the Ashiana workshop shows how twenty MarketPlace artisans actively took on and overcame a challenge. Formerly part of a larger NGO, the women were subservient to a man who managed the group, while keeping all business transactions private and tightly under his control. After the women repeatedly complained to Fatima Merchant, SHARE director, she challenged the women to leave the NGO and form their own group. However, little action followed as the women claimed they could not come up with the 1,000-rupee ($22 US) per-member start-up funds required by MarketPlace for new group formation. Exasperated, Fatima "put it on the line" by giving the women a deadline to collect the money or the group was "finished." Practically overnight, the women rallied together, pawned their jewelry, borrowed small sums from family members, and came up with the necessary funds. After receiving a matching loan from MarketPlace, Ashiana was under way. In the ensuing month, the members learned to plan orders, purchase fabric, buy sewing machines, use the telephone, ride the bus, open a bank account, write checks, and make deliveries—everything that the former leader had kept from them.

Across all seven workshops, the set of production skills acquired by MarketPlace artisans provides a strong foundation of capacity for producing garments at acceptable levels of quality and in a timely manner for the international market. These skills advance the artisans to new levels of professionalism, beyond sewing or embroidering for their personal needs. More specifically, artisans acquire capabilities that allow them to

- produce to specifications,

- understand differences in cross-cultural consumer preference and the necessity of producing to customer demand,

- develop production-planning schedules,

- establish workplace efficiencies,

- apply creativity in solving production problems and completing orders when emergencies arise, and

- cooperate in contributing to a total group effort.

Communication and Interpersonal Capabilities: Reaching Beyond the Workshops

As MarketPlace artisans acquire production capabilities, concomitant communication and interpersonal skills emerge for application both within and outside the workshops (see Table 5.1). For well over one-half of the women, leaving the immediate vicinities of their homes to pick up MarketPlace work, make deliveries, and conduct workshop business outside the slum are first-time occurrences. Travel may require several hours to complete the tasks. Learning to use public transportation becomes a vital skill. For many women, riding the train or bus for the first time was frightening. One woman shared that on her first bus ride, she rode around for five hours as she didn't know how to read the signs to get off. Women proudly relate, "Now, I can travel anywhere in Bombay by myself."

Learning to use the telephone was equally challenging, with half of the women making telephone calls for the first time in their roles as MarketPlace artisans. Women recall their first telephone experiences by demonstrating how they held the phones upside down or backward when trying to initiate a call. Determining whose voice was coming out of the telephone was particularly puzzling at first. Today cell phones are ubiquitous among workshop leaders.

As women become active in their workshops, they learn how to speak openly with their fellow artisans, conduct meetings, offer opinions, and become leaders. Cultural norms of female shyness and subservience, supported by husbands and in-laws, have permeated artisans' lives prior to joining MarketPlace. However, as women are encouraged to speak up at workshop training and meetings, confidence emerges. Several artisans share observations of MarketPlace artisan colleagues.

> There was one woman who didn't know how to ask for help when she didn't know how to do a certain stitch. Now she is not afraid to ask and is one of the best teachers.

> The ladies who come to work for Udan Mandal, initially they are very shy. These women sit in the corner and are quiet. Now after it has been a while, they are like lions.

> People have become brave and learned to speak up. Many of the women are from a part of India where it is very conservative. They have come to realize that if they don't work to make their life better, who else will do it for them?

Women not only observe newfound strength in other women but also take great pride in their own newly acquired confidence.

> I believe in myself and can do whatever comes in my way.

> I have become very independent. My personality has changed overall. I never depend on anyone financially.

> I can stand on my own two feet, which I never thought possible before I started working with MarketPlace. With the tension at home, I am less scared now that I work so hard and make money for myself. I am able to be more open with others . . . speak my mind more openly.

Confidence gained in the MarketPlace workshops parlays into courage as women apply their new capabilities in taking greater responsibility for their lives and that of their children.

> My husband wouldn't allow me to apply for a ration card. After he died I applied and received a card. So now I can feed my children better. The ladies told me that I had to cook food every day; previously I did not do this. I am very proud to carry a ration card.

> When I go to my husband's native place, I speak up to my mother-in-law and tell her she needs to treat my children nicely. I tell her I am here to protect my children.

> I have the strength to solve my own problems and I have become very courageous. I had several children and had an abortion when I conceived

another child because I knew it would be hard to raise another child. My husband didn't know. This is an example of my courage.

I take care of my children but I also take care of myself, as I am the only parent. At MarketPlace, we are urged to take care of ourselves and our children . . . as well as our work.

At first I used to think, how will I take responsibility for educating my children. But I did . . . in English medium. I am very satisfied. I have played the role of father as well as mother.

Artisans not only apply their new capabilities in their own households, but also join together in helping other women learn new skills or solve their problems. Artisans describe two examples of support offered among MarketPlace artisans.

Right from the beginning, some women did not know how to read or write. They did not have confidence to express their opinions. We held classes in health and all passed. We helped each other study for the exam. It was very exciting.

Once there was a woman who had children and it was too hard for her to handle. We told her to get an operation so that she could have more time for herself and her family and she did. Now things are better for her.

As the women began acquiring capabilities that were changing their lives, they expressed interest that their children share in the learning. Pushpika describes the women's request to her.

Through their work with MarketPlace, [the artisans] found the strength to change, make a difference and influence the community around them. I was satisfied with this outcome until the women posed another challenge. They wanted their children to be empowered, also. They asked that their sons and daughters learn how to deal with life, become responsible citizens and continue to bring about the change they had started.

This made so much sense that the Armaan Club program [see Chapter 3] found a new perspective. The Armaan Club originally began to supplement experiences and learning that the artisans' children did not get in their classroom. Now the program is taking it further. It will identify six to eight children from each group and divide them into two age levels: ages six to twelve and ages thirteen to eighteen. These children will be given leadership training and will learn various life skills. Then they will take what they've learned and share it with the other children in their groups. The older kids will be trained on issues like AIDS, hygiene, human rights and responsibilities, and will then develop street plays that they will perform in the various communities.

In summary, women who rarely left their homes except to accompany their children to school are now speaking up and taking control in their households without asking or checking with others. Learning to use the telephone and board public transportation opens the artisans to a world beyond their homes and slums. Tasks such as going out to buy vegetables, selecting a new sari, sending a child to a better school, making a reproductive choice, or going to the hospital for her own health needs are first-time undertakings for women long under the influence of their husbands or his extended family. Cultural norms of shyness and submissiveness disappear as women acquire self-respect and confidence not only to solve their own problems but to help others as well.

Comparison of All-Female and Mixed-Gender Groups

Cultural expectations about gender and work led us to examine artisans' perspectives on the gender composition of their workshops. Artisans' responses highlighted differences related to broader social issues as well as to production planning and completion of work. Members of the three all-female groups see many advantages to this type of group. Advantages include the following:

- Freedom to work outside the house

- Opportunities for talking freely with each other

- Helping each other face their problems

- Achieving empowerment and reduced dependence on men

All-female groups offer some women an opportunity to work outside the home that they would otherwise be denied. This is especially true for Muslim women whose families are traditionally very protective. For example, one woman explained that

> If Ashiana included men, I would not be allowed to work for them. It is essential that it is all women. Because it is only women, husbands trust Ashiana with their women and also allow the children to go on the picnics they arrange.

Other women, though not completely restricted from working, would have some limitations put on their work if the group was mixed-gender. One woman reported that

> If men worked with us, I would not stay late into the day at the workshop. I would only feel comfortable working at home and my husband would not approve otherwise.

Another commonly perceived advantage is that the all-female group offers women the freedom to be completely open with their speech and behaviors in the workplace. In all-female groups, women enjoy talking about anything. They feel that they can be themselves and openly share their problems with each other. Two women explained,

> We can speak freely because there are no men. After speaking about my problems to others, my heart is calm.

> It's like a family. We believe in peace. We share views and opinions. I can't talk about things at home. It's so different than at home.

Women who are members of all-female groups also view this freedom as an advantage because by talking to each other, women can provide support for each other and aid in solving each other's problems. One woman offered that

> Arpan is all women. I like it that the women are my friends. They don't hurt me. We surround each other with a supporting atmosphere.

Another woman commented on the healing power of an all-female group, stating that

> We can talk about whatever problems we have. There is nothing we can't talk about. We get ideas and solutions for our problems. We forget our tensions.

When discussing the advantages of all-women versus mixed-gender groups, women artisans also noted that men often do not take into consideration certain women's needs. As an example they described a group member who is HIV positive and very weak. The group members save work for her to make sure that she receives some income.

Personal problem solving that occurs with the all-female groups applies to many workshop issues as well. Women reported that an advantage of being part of an all-female group is that the women lessen their dependence on men, "If men were in the group, we would go to the men and be dependent on the men for the answers." With no men to lean on, the women take responsibility for mastering all the tasks of the work, including heavy lifting and traveling about the city. One woman told a story of her experience,

> One time I had to deliver 450 jackets and, when arriving at the toll station coming south from Thane, a police officer asked me what I was doing and where I got the products. He wanted 1,700 rupees as a bribe so I said, "OK take my pieces" but of course he wanted money. So I finally paid a bribe of twenty rupees. Now the Arpan group laughs about the situation and says "what a great woman you are!"

Taking charge of other outside jobs further severs the dependence women have on men. For example, one woman explained that

> If there were men, the job of collecting the fabric would have been given to them. We would not have the courage to go out and do it ourselves, but we are doing all the work.

Further explaining the empowerment that women in all-female groups experience, one artisan stated,

> We can prove that we don't need men to solve our problems. Whether they are small or big, we realize that they are OUR problems and we must make them better.

Another woman offered simply that

> I like it that all ladies can handle everything. If there were men, they would issue orders and the women would come to depend on them.

In contrast with all-women workshops, artisans belonging to mixed-gender groups also see advantages with this arrangement, including the following:

- Men can be depended on to handle outside work and problems that come up.
- Brotherly and trustful relationships where the women feel equal and respected can be maintained.

- Privacy between the sexes can be offered by allotting separate workspaces.

While the all-female groups took pride in their independence, ironically, a dependence on men is seen as an advantage by some women belonging to mixed-gender groups. In these workplaces, men routinely take charge of certain work tasks that are viewed as "men's work." For example, two artisans commented,

> Men can do the difficult work like cutting, carrying heavy things, getting things done that require going outside, and they can work all night if they need to.

> The men do the cutting faster. It is a hard job so I like it.

However, the dependence on men goes beyond assignment of certain work tasks. Those in mixed-gender groups thought that it was advantageous to have men around to act in leadership roles when the supervisor was away. Yet, the easy availability of men in the workplace seems to diminish the resourcefulness of women. Two artisans provided understanding of this situation, explaining that

> If we have any difficulties solving problems with the patterns, the men help out. And when the supervisor isn't there, the men help out with work problems.

> When there are difficulties and the women can't solve them, first they go to the men and then, if the men can't explain the problems, they go to the supervisor.

Although lacking in some opportunities to expand empowerment and create independence, being involved in a mixed group may provide some of the women who are most disillusioned with men an opportunity to experience trustful relationships with men. Being part of a mixed-gender group is like being part of a family where the male workers are viewed as brothers. Commenting positively on her experiences with mixed-gender groups, one artisan offered that

> We have a familial relationship. They are like my brothers. Before, I could not talk to men and now I can. I feel confident in talking with men.

In further support of a mixed-gender workshop, an artisan pointed to a photo she took for the photoelicitation interview, where she is talking with her male supervisor. She notes that she is now comfortable talking with men and in fact has become quite bold.

The interactions with women in the workplace may also be beneficial in that men begin to treat women with more equality. Toward this end, one artisan reported, "I have achieved equality with everyone. A lot of equality is maintained in working together." Finally, privacy between the sexes can still be maintained with mixed-gender groups. With its two-floor workshop, WARE creates a physical separation in the workplace that allows men and women to maintain distance from each other.

That the MarketPlace men recognize the need to learn how to interact and speak with women co-supervisors they requested that intergender communication be a topic for CACTUS (Care and Concern Toward Us) (former men-only support group, see Chapter 3) discussion. Women supervisors were asked to join the discussion about workplace communication. Following this request, women supervisors have remained as CACTUS members.

Entrepreneurial Applications: Offshoot Businesses (With Susan Strawn, PhD)[3]

As noted in Chapter 2, Amartya Sen (1993), a development economist, argues that workers in poor countries need not only access to training and technology but also opportunities to apply their newly acquired skills. MarketPlace artisans present two examples of entrepreneurial application of capabilities through developing offshoot businesses. Both are examples of supervisors—three males and one female—who pursued new business opportunities that built upon technical and business skills acquired at MarketPlace.

Indian Roots

Beginning in 1998, three MarketPlace supervisors seized the opportunity to apply what they had learned as production leaders for their workshops. The new business arm within MarketPlace caters to a local customer base. Indian Roots leaders Aburkani Mohmed (Sahara), Abdul Sheikh (Ghar Udyog), and Neenah Sikhligar (Udan Mandal) forged a business plan that has generated additional work for MarketPlace artisans while protecting the distinctive MarketPlace "look" for their export market. MarketPlace requires that its fabric suppliers retain for at least two years all custom-dyed and printed fabric that has been rejected for inaccurate color or printing. After the requisite waiting period, Indian Roots purchases at cost the rejected fabric for artisans to tailor and embroider into Indian Roots products. This arrangement places fabrics used in the Indian Roots product line three seasons behind the MarketPlace catalog.

Indian Roots sells small orders to a government shop but relies heavily on one annual sale in Mumbai. Concern India, an organization that coordinates exhibitions and sales of Indian handicrafts in government halls, stages a three-day sale each November during Diwali, the Hindu festival of lights for which many Indians purchase new clothes. MarketPlace artisans prepare for the sale by tailoring and embroidering Indian Roots products during times when MarketPlace orders are slow. The month before the sale, however, they intensify their efforts for Indian Roots. When Indian Roots sells out during the first day of the Concern India sale, artisans work through the night sewing and embroidering more products to sell the next day. Indian Roots pays artisans in cash at the same rate as MarketPlace.

These business leaders have applied their marketing expertise of producing to customer demand as they adjust styles for the Indian Roots product line according to preferences of Indian consumers who buy at Concern India. Indian Roots sells wrap skirts, blouses, pants, and the loose-fitting Indian tops called kurtas and salwars at the Concern India sale. Most Indian customers will not buy jackets and vests, prevalent in the MarketPlace export line, because they cannot wear them over local garment styles. The Indian Roots leaders also adjust production time for surface embellishment as a way to reduce prices to an affordable level for Indian customers. Typically, an artisan embroiders six hours on one MarketPlace garment, but prices for an Indian Roots product sold at Concern India will support only one hour of embroidery.

During January 2003, Indian Roots took on a new marketing challenge. The Earthwatch Institute volunteers and researchers for our project became their first group of non-Indian customers. During the Earthwatch orientation sessions at the MarketPlace office, volunteers from Australia, Canada, England, and the United States sifted through racks and tables that held clothing, household textiles, tote bags, business card files, and computer disk holders. Watching for products that became bestsellers, Indian Roots business leaders brought new products on ensuing days for their enthusiastic Earthwatch customers. Neenah and Aburkani used their eye for design and suggested fabric and style combinations for customer orders from the overseas visitors. Based on this initial success with Earthwatch volunteers,

Indian Roots now makes sure to have products available for the increasing number of tourist groups that visit MarketPlace to learn about fair trade.

These business leaders, who learned their production skills in Market-Place workshops, have transferred their technical and marketing expertise to Indian Roots. They conduct informal market research by monitoring customer purchases, design to customer demand, deliver fabric and materials to workshops, train artisans in production techniques, maintain quality standards, deliver finished products to appropriate venues, market garments at sales, and distribute payment to artisans.

Udog Kala Kendra

The second artisan enterprise that grew from MarketPlace is Udog Kala Kendra, a fabric dyeing and surface embellishment workshop. P. Ziauddin (Zia), who joined MarketPlace in the late 1980s, used dye and fabric-printing skills he learned at MarketPlace to develop his business. Initially, all MarketPlace fabric was contracted to outside firms in northwest India, an overnight train ride away. Sourcing fabrics in a timely manner was difficult. In addition, when fabrics arrived, they sometimes had to be overdyed when contract dyers failed to meet Marketplace's color specifications. Overdyeing became Zia's responsibility.

Zia observed the problem of unreliable fabric production and used his emerging skills as a dyer to start a new workshop in Utan, a quiet seaside village forty miles north of Mumbai. Along with ten employees, he dyes and prints fabric exclusive to the seasonal MarketPlace colors and motifs that he guards with care. The production accounts for approximately 40 to 50 percent of the fabric MarketPlace purchases. Zia's workshop handles many surface design treatments, including tie-dye, batik, and overdyeing. Shehnaz Sheikh, the only woman in the workshop, paints delicate freehand designs in pale yellow wax, some of which are her own, onto the borders of undyed curtains and tailored salwars. Zia's business has prospered. In 2003, he moved his workshop into a newly purchased building, four times the size of his rented space. With a large wax reservoir built into the workshop floor, Zia is positioned to further expand fabric production.

In these two entrepreneurial ventures, artisan managers have drawn upon a range of capabilities acquired at MarketPlace. First, business leaders gained thorough knowledge of textile production techniques by working in a fair trade organization that shared rather than protected technical expertise. This knowledge, in turn, positioned them to train their own artisan employees, maintain specialized equipment, and source appropriate raw materials.

Second, business leaders gained an understanding of the role of innovation and change in the market by observing the carefully guarded alternations in seasonal styles and motifs at MarketPlace. Their new entrepreneurial ventures reflect a spirit of innovation and change appropriate to their intended domestic and export markets. Third, business leaders garnered skills for managing people and production as they were given increasing responsibility in overall production planning and execution at MarketPlace.

Artisan Work: Survival or Asset-Building Strategies

We return to the question posed by development practitioners: Are artisan enterprises merely a survival strategy or are they also contributing to asset building? The business, communication, and interpersonal capabilities described in this chapter suggest that when an artisan enterprise is dedicated to transparent sharing of business practices and to artisan development, artisan employees build assets for active participation in the marketplace. They learn to communicate with others and, as they travel outside the slum, gain awareness of choices for their lives. Passive acceptance of life evolves into self-respect and active decision making for themselves, their children, and fellow artisans. New entrepreneurial enterprises arise as artisans take risks and reach out to new target markets. The MarketPlace artisans answer affirmatively that profitable business practices and asset-building strategies can coincide. In the next chapter we address the first part of the question as to whether artisan work can also contribute to economic livelihood.

Notes

1. The analysis in this chapter is based on a series of interview questions, including the following:

- Since coming to [name of workshop], what sewing or embroidery skills have you learned that have improved your work? How do you work differently now than before?
- Since coming to MarketPlace, what else have you learned beyond your tailoring/embroidery skills that is important to you in your life? (answered through a list of topics)
- Have you ever had a time when it was difficult for you to complete your order? What were the circumstances and how did you meet the challenge?
- As you think about the members of [name of workshop], what are the most important changes you see in the other members' lives as you look around you?

2. Production planning involves application of mathematical skills for completing an order of a given magnitude, given a specific delivery date. At a minimum, calculations must take into consideration the number of artisans, time for completion of each production task, sequencing of tailoring and embroidery tasks, production capabilities per artisan, and projected date for delivery.

3. For a full version of the article from which this section is drawn, see Strawn, S., and Littrell, M. A. 2006. Beyond capabilities: A case study of three artisan enterprises in India. *Clothing and Textiles Research Journal,* 24 no. 3: 207-213.

CHAPTER 6

Economic Livelihood of
MarketPlace Artisans

I have a friend whose husband was a drunkard ... but now she can support her family and her kids because she has her own money.

I am becoming more financially stable. I do not have to ask anyone for money.

Our income is now higher and more stable.

T he experiences of the women described above were recounted by MarketPlace artisans when they responded to our questions about the most important changes they had seen in their own lives and those of the other members of their groups. Their responses express the power that is gained when a woman is able to provide for herself and her family with her own earnings. This chapter describes the economic livelihood gained by artisans who work with MarketPlace: Handwork of India. In it, we detail the wages the workers earn. We consider reasons for the apparent underemployment of the artisans. We also describe the wages that are pooled among household members to cover household expenses. We outline the primary household expenditures, including those covering the most basic of needs. Next, a variety of measures to assess the adequacy of artisan remuneration are examined. The views of artisans about whether they feel the pay they receive is fair for the work they complete are also presented. Finally, we explore differences in economic livelihood between the groups working with MarketPlace.[1]

Economic Livelihood From Artisan Wages

Economic livelihood is required for material well-being and is gained from a dependable source of cash and food to meet basic needs. Economic livelihood can be gained as a result of noncash resources that are obtained through activities like raising animals and gardening, or receiving gifts of agricultural products from family members who have greater access to these resources. Approximately 43 percent of MarketPlace artisans have grown up in Mumbai, a large city that provides limited opportunities for gardening and raising livestock. The remaining 57 percent of artisans have migrated from rural areas throughout the country to reside in this urban area of Mumbai for reasons such as marriage or to look for work. Infrequent visits to the familial home or "native place" offer few opportunities to reap the harvests of their families. Thus, not surprisingly, economic livelihood for the MarketPlace artisans is primarily based on wages from work and only two out of every ten artisans reported receiving small gifts of grains, sweets, or other resources from friends and family.

MarketPlace artisans average 5.3 years of experience working with the organization. The artisans are paid wages for the number of pieces sewn or embroidered, so their incomes fluctuate from month to month based on the amount of work available and the time and effort each artisan puts into production. This seasonal variability not only is typical to the apparel industry but also emanates from the unique production delays arising from MarketPlace's commitment to using small groups and handcrafted fabrics. Seasonal variability contributes to short bursts of heavy production at some times of the year where most artisans, who share a commitment to the success of their groups, work seven days a week and longer hours each day to meet deadlines. Yet, at other times of the year, there is very light production, when artisans sit idle for several weeks at a time. Overall, the artisans' average monthly income was 1,428 rupees.[2] In months when work was slow, artisans' salaries averaged 1,110 rupees. During these slow months, 54.1 percent of artisans indicated that they earned between 500 and 1,000 rupees. This remuneration is equivalent to only 35 to 70 percent of the average monthly salary; thus, it represents a significant drop in spending power. In contrast, during months with heavier production, salaries averaged 1,746 rupees. The type of job held by the artisans makes a significant difference in the wages that are earned. The wages earned by tailors were consistently 35 to 36 percent higher than embroiderers' wages during both heavy and light work times, and when incomes were averaged (see Table 6.1).

Table 6.1 Monthly wages by job type (in rupees)

ARTISAN MONTHLY WAGES	TAILORS	EMBROIDERERS	COMBINED
Average of heavy and light production	1,779	1,314	1,428
Average during light production	1,376	1,010	1,110
Average during heavy production	2,181	1,618	1,746

A discussion of artisan wages is incomplete without understanding how the wage rates are set. Pushpika describes the process of determining the prices paid to the groups for the garments as starting with the calculation of costs for all raw materials, including yarn, fabrics, and buttons. For determining labor costs, time studies are conducted in the MarketPlace Bombay office using artisans having average skill levels—not really slow and not really quick. The time taken to complete a piece is then used to determine a piece-rate that will provide a minimum wage. Because MarketPlace has several basic garment styles they continue each season, it is only necessary to conduct time studies to determine wages for tailoring when a new style is introduced. In contrast, time studies are routinely carried out for determining embroidery piece rates, due to the designs changing frequently. When the World of Good's fair trade calculator described in Chapter 2 was developed, MarketPlace used it to verify that wages paid were above all the standards used in the calculator. The rate of pay for tailors and embroiderers is adjusted to be equal. MarketPlace aims for both jobs to return a rate of twenty-eight rupees per hour. The organization expects and follows up with each artisan group to ensure that this hourly rate is met by its artisans.

While there are no minimum wage requirements in India for home-based sewing and embroidery, minimum wages for garment industry tailors were 2,843 rupees per month in 2002 (including allowances added to cover inflation) over a regular work week of six days and forty-eight hours (R. Majumdar, personal communication, Asia Administrator, Fair Labor Association September 8). Considering the basis from which MarketPlace and the groups set wages, if artisans were fully employed, working forty hours per week, the average rate of pay would equal 4,320 rupees per month—well over the most relevant legal minimum wage. However, the average monthly income of 1,779 rupees for tailors fell short of meeting this minimum wage requirement when averaging light and heavy production times, and even when production was at its heaviest. We believe this shortfall is primarily due to there being too little work to provide most of the artisans with full employment, not that the rate of pay per hour is inadequate. We attempted to confirm this by determining the number of hours artisans were working, but despite using two different questions directly asking artisans about their working hours, their self-reports were highly variable and of questionable validity. While each group maintains records of the pieces completed by each artisan and their pay for those pieces, records are not kept on hours worked; thus, there were no formal documents that could be examined. The lack of formal documentation of working hours is not unusual in cottage industries in developing countries or with work conducted at home in developed countries.

Despite the difficulty measuring hours worked, we did gain some tentative impressions about the patterns in artisans' working hours and their visits to the central workshop.

- Most tailors carry out work at their group's central workplace, visiting the workplace six days a week, and staying for several hours even when orders are light and can be completed in shorter periods of time. Thus, the rate of productivity varies by the amount of work available, increasing when orders are heavy and decreasing when orders are light.

- Embroiderers come to their groups' central workplaces to pick up work, but nearly all embroidery work is completed at home and, as described in Chapter 4, is managed around a range of household duties across a day. Because of the small blocks of time available to embroiderers for nonhousehold work, the women often spread their work out throughout the week, completing at least a little work each day. When there is plenty of work, artisans are likely embroidering five or six hours per day.

- The way that household duties and embroidery work are intermingled throughout the day makes it difficult for artisans to accurately track hours worked each day.

- The central workplace is a place to socialize with others in the group and to participate in social action projects and other development activities, which also complicates tracking of actual work hours.

Reasons for Artisan Underemployment

Underemployment refers to situations where workers are employed in less than full-time work, which seems to describe the situation of many of the artisans we interviewed. There are many reasons we believe underemployment is observed among those sewing and embroidering for MarketPlace. First, there is currently not enough demand from US customers for Market-Place products to keep all the artisans busy at full-time levels. Second, limitations on mobility prevent some workers from working full-time. For example, women with very young children would have few options in the slums for childcare if they pursued artisan work on a full-time basis. Third, members of the various workshops have chosen to partially assist a larger number of artisans, rather than to fully employ a smaller number of artisans. The outcomes of this choice are most clearly reflected in the fact that embroiderers tend to underearn tailors, even though the wage rates for each job are set the same. Embroidery work can be carried out by women with very limited skills, thus where there is a desire to help more individuals with work, the ranks of those doing embroidery are increased and the orders distributed to a larger number of artisans. We did observe, however, a positive correlation between minimum and maximum artisan wages meaning that individuals who earned the most money when orders were light also made the most when orders were heavy, suggesting that there is a core of more productive artisans that are relied on most heavily to complete orders while other artisans who are less productive are provided some work in hopes of meeting at least some of their basic needs. Finally, it is likely that many of the women would choose part-time work over full-time work if it was available. As we outlined in Chapter 4, the household duties among these Indian women are time-consuming and never-ending.

Total Household Income

Typically, the wages earned by the artisans are but one of the sources of income their households receive. Total household income, determined by adding the reported wages of the artisan, spouse, and other household earners, averaged 4,168 rupees though the total income ranged widely from only 500 rupees to 11,650 rupees monthly. The share of the total household income contributed by the artisan averaged 40 percent, but depending on the household ranged from 3 percent to 100 percent of total household income.

Eight artisans were the sole source of income for their households; however, on average 2.33 people contributed income.[3] The total household income was used to cover the expenses of households that averaged 5.22 people, but ranged in size from one member to a joint family of thirteen persons.

The artisans' spouses were frequently an important source of household income, accounting for an average of 48 percent of the total household income. The income earned by spouses, who averaged 2,043 rupees, tended to be substantially greater than that of the artisans.[4] Yet, almost 20 percent of spouses living in the household did not contribute any money on a monthly basis. Women artisans explained their spouses' unemployment as stemming primarily from alcoholism, an illness or injury, or lack of motivation. Accidents and life-threatening diseases, such as diabetes and tuberculosis, were noted by several women as preventing their husbands from working. One woman explained that her husband is lazy and works as he pleases, sharing with us that

___is very lazy and causes difficulty in the household due to this serious stubbornness.

Another woman shared her family situation.

> My husband has not worked in six months … In good times he has
> made 5000 rupees per month. I don't understand what is going on right
> now. He says that people aren't ordering, or paying, but the workers
> call him and ask for him to come to work but he does not go. He seems
> to be depending on my income. I don't know the inside story.

In addition to spouses, for 44 percent of households there was at least one
additional household member contributing income for household expenses.
For the married artisans, this was often a brother-in-law or unmarried adult
child. For single artisans, fathers or other siblings sometimes earned wages to
help with family expenses. On average, members of the household beyond
the artisan and spouse contributed total monthly income of 1,027 rupees;
however, the wages added by additional household members ranged from
50 to 18,000 rupees per month.[5] Thus, the presence of an additional wage
earner in some cases offset only the higher food costs associated with the
additional mouth, but in other cases made a tremendous impact on what
the household could afford.

An additional source of economic livelihood was from nonwage earnings,
such as renting space in the home. Only 10.6 percent of artisans reported
having another source of income beyond wages earned by those living in
their households. This additional amount averaged 319 rupees per month,
but both the median and mode for this variable were zero. Because it affected
so few artisans, we did not include these data into the calculation of average
total household income.

Household Expenditures

How far can an average total household income of only 4,168 rupees be
stretched? An inventory of household expenditures provided an understanding of the extent that income is adequate to cover basic needs and how it is
distributed among various expenditure categories (see Figure 6.1).[6] For most
artisan families, food, transportation, and utilities (water, cooking fuel, and
electricity) were recurring monthly expenditures. As is typical in developing
countries, the greatest expenditures were for food (68.8 percent of total basic
expenditures). This statistic corresponds with Engel's law that household
income negatively correlates to proportion of total expenditures devoted to
food. In developing countries, the portion of expenditures devoted to food is
often over 50 percent (Traill 1999). Previous studies of expenditures in India
have found the percentage spent on food has dropped between 1972-1973

Figure 6.1 Expenditures on Basic Minimum Needs (in rupees).

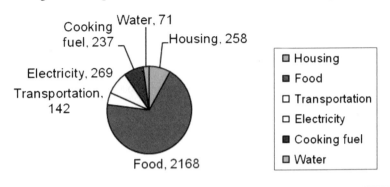

Cooking fuel, 237

Water, 71

Housing, 258

Electricity, 269

Transportation, 142

Food, 2168

- Housing
- Food
- Transportation
- Electricity
- Cooking fuel
- Water

and 2004-2005 from 73 percent to 55 percent in rural areas, and from 65 percent to 43 percent in urban areas (Srinivas 2008).

Expenditures for food varied from nothing, for one person who lived alone and was provided for by friends, to 7,000 rupees per month. The median monthly expenditure for food was 2,000 rupees and 53.5 percent spent between 1,500 and 3,000 rupees per month on food. A weak correlation between expenditures on food and household size suggests that larger amounts of money spent on food were due only somewhat to family size. It is likely that some relatively small families are eating higher quality or a greater quantity of food.[7]

Housing expenditures were surprising as we had initially anticipated that every household would incur some housing costs. However, a large proportion of artisan families (54 percent) had no monthly expense for housing because they "owned" their homes and had no mortgage. It is possible that the higher proportion we found to be spent on food could be a result of the very low housing expenditures made by many families. The large number of households having no housing expenditures probably leads to an underestimation of the needed money for housing among those who rent or have a mortgage. While 10.6 percent of households paid 200 or fewer rupees monthly for housing, 20.5 percent paid from 258 to 1,000 rupees per month on their living accommodations.

Pushpika Freitas provided further insight into home expenditures.

It is extremely difficult to get out of the slums. Instead the home becomes less and less makeshift. People add concrete to the floor versus mud, metal sheets for the roof as opposed to leaves. The roadside homes are the most makeshift and many of the women started this way.

Regarding home ownership, Pushpika further explained that

> You are buying the right to occupy the space, but the land itself belongs to the government. There would be a riot if the government tried to take it back. So the government has a situation where you can occupy the space—you don't own it. And when you sell you are selling the right to occupy the space. Owners continue to make improvements on their homes because it is too expensive to buy housing outside the slums.

Taken together, expenditures on electricity, cooking fuel, and water totaled an average of 575 rupees per month and were relatively stable compared to some of the other expenses. Nearly 48 percent of households had no transportation costs because they either walked or took advantage of a household member's employment as an autorickshaw driver, thus catching free rides when necessary. Rupees set aside for entertainment were virtually nonexistent. The type of entertainment enjoyed on an average of fifty-seven rupees per month would be an occasional ice cream cone or other sweet for the children.

Some expenditure categories were widely varied in the amounts artisan households spent annually. While the median expenditure for medications and medical services was 1,080 rupees annually, the much higher mean of 2,110 was influenced by the 17.6 percent of households spending from 4,000 to 18,000 rupees as they fought off cancer, polio, or other life-threatening medical problems. These high medical expenditures revealed the willingness to assume great debt to obtain higher quality (and higher cost) health care from private hospitals when families faced a medical crisis.

While public education is free in India, there are expenses for buying children the required uniforms and books, and transporting them to school. Nearly 24 percent of the artisan households reported no expenses for school tuition. However, an average of 530 rupees was spent on educating children each month and 14.5 percent of households spent at least 1,000 rupees or more per month. Each artisan had an average of three children; the range was from zero to ten children. The relatively large amount spent for education by some families probably reflects the high priority some households placed on educating children in English medium schools; these schools charge tuition of all students and are difficult to get into, and yet are more desirable than public schools using the local Indian language. Other highly variable expenditures included those made for clothing and travel to visit family in other parts of the country.

Assessing the Adequacy of Earnings: Basic Minimum Needs, Living Wages, and Fair Pay

It is difficult to understand the value of earnings without addressing whether the income is adequate for covering a household's fundamental needs for survival, which we term "Basic Minimum Needs." To determine the artisan families' Basic Minimum Needs, we summed monthly expenditures for housing, food, transportation, and utilities (electricity, cooking fuel, and water). We did not include costs for educating children in the calculation of basic expenditures because it was possible for children to be educated at no expense. Basic Minimum Needs for housing, food, transportation, and utilities averaged 3,145 rupees per month.[8] Fifty percent of artisan households required from 2,528 to 3,955 rupees monthly for these basic expenditures.

To understand more about how well the artisans and other household members' earnings covered their most basic needs, we calculated a Basic Minimum Needs Ratio by dividing each household's monthly total household income by its average monthly Basic Minimum Needs. The ratio represents the extent that total household income was sufficient to cover the basic expenditures. When the result of the calculation was 1.0 or greater, the average monthly income was sufficient for covering these needs and some other expenses. However, when the ratio resulted in a score of less than 1.0, the household income did not cover the most basic of expenditures for housing, food, transportation, and utilities.

The mean for the Basic Minimum Needs ratio was 1.48, showing that on average families were able to cover their Basic Minimum Needs with the available income. However, the range for this measure was from 0.19 to 5.34 and 27.4 percent of artisan households had scores of less than 1.0, indicating that they were unable to cover these basic needs with their monthly incomes.[9] These households are clearly at risk and impoverished.

To understand more about the households that were unable to meet their basic needs, we compared them with those households that were able to meet their Basic Minimum Needs on a variety of household and work-related variables.[10] The ability to meet Basic Minimum Needs did not improve or decline depending on whether the artisan embroiders or sews for MarketPlace, nor whether they had been employed with MarketPlace for a short or long time. What distinguished between households that were able to meet their needs and those unable to do so was the variability of wages earned by the spouse, and others in the household. Spouses and others' wages varied widely in the monthly earnings they contributed. The higher the wages earned by spouses and others in the household, the more likely the household was able to meet its basic needs. Yet, when spouses and others earned low wages, their households were increasingly unlikely to cover their most basic needs.[11] Although not enough to cover all the households' needs, artisans' wages were making important contributions because 61 percent of households would fall short of covering their Basic Minimum Needs without the these earnings.[12] These findings point to the critical need for multiple earners in the household and the stability that is contributed by artisans' work. To be successful, it is necessary for artisans, their spouses, and often other household members to be fully employed.

These findings also highlight the difficulties that MarketPlace artisans who are sole earners in their households are likely to face in providing the support needed by their families; however, only six artisans fell into that category. Ten artisans (28.6 percent) that were single or widowed were unable to meet their Basic Minimum Needs with their own earnings; however, all but two had additional sources of income within the household. Another four women who were married were sole earners for their households and two of those were unable to meet Basic Minimum Needs with their earnings. While the women working with MarketPlace are making significant contributions to household income, it is extremely difficult for a sole earner to cover the needs of the entire family.

Living Wages

Living wage is an additional concept for understanding what minimum compensation is needed by workers to obtain a dignified level of living. The Asia Floor Wage for India has been calculated to be 6,969 rupees, which is meant to cover the total needs of a family of two adults and two children (Asia Floor Wage Alliance Campaign 2009). It is important to note that the Asia Floor Wage and other calculations of living wages assume workers are fully employed, which it appears MarketPlace artisans are not. Thus, it is not surprising that even in the heaviest periods of production, the 1,746 rupees that artisans were making as average salary was less than 23 percent of this standard. We calculated an absolute minimal living wage that would be necessary for MarketPlace artisans using the average expenditures of 3,145 rupees plus 10 percent savings that were needed to cover Basic Minimum Needs for food, housing, transportation, and utilities, divided by the average 2.3 adult wage earners in the household to determine whether their remuneration might meet this more modest estimate of living wage that assumes more workers are contributing wages to cover household expenses. To adequately cover the artisan's share of household expenditures plus savings required wages of at least 1,500 rupees per month. According to average pay (1,428 rupees), artisans are close to earning this living wage, even in light of their underemployment. When earnings from slow and high production are averaged out, 44 percent of artisans earn at this living wage level. During months with slow production, the proportion of artisans earning the living wage drops to 30 percent. However, 62 percent of artisans are able to earn a living wage when production is at its peak.

We examined several variables to see if those earning the living wage had different work patterns or personal characteristics than those not earning the living wage. Those earning and not earning a living wage had similar length of tenure with MarketPlace, as well as similar levels of educational attainment. What differed between those earning the living wage and those not earning at this rate was their job type. Over 58 percent of the tailors received a living wage, whereas just 38 percent of embroiderers received this wage level.[13] This finding provides further evidence that workshops are making altruistic decisions to spread out the work to larger numbers of individuals so as to assist more households. It is easier to provide embroidery work to unskilled artisans in need of wages than it is to provide more skill-intensive tailoring work to those individuals lacking the requisite skills.

Relationships to Standards With the Wage Ladder

To provide guidance to MarketPlace and its groups for evaluating their artisan wages in relationship to various standards, we plotted wage data on a wage ladder (see Figure 6.2). The wage ladder visually represents where MarketPlace artisans' wages fall in relation to the most relevant legal minimum wage, our calculated living wage, and the Asia Floor Wage. The floor of each box indicates where the minimum artisan's wages fall on the ladder while the top of each box aligns with the highest wages earned by an artisan. The mean and median wages are marked by lines within each box.

As indicated in the wage ladder, wages earned by a relatively large proportion of artisans during light production fall short of meeting the most relevant legal minimum wage or our calculated living wage. During heavy production, the average workers' wages approximately meet living wages. All workers' wages fall short of meeting the Asia Floor Wage of 6,969 rupees that has been calculated for India. The groups may find this fair wage ladder to be useful in tracking progress on wages and determining when it is appropriate to expand the number of artisans in a workshop. For example, groups could monitor the wages of artisans on a wage ladder and could refrain from employing additional artisans until the living wage was achieved by all artisans desiring full-time work.

Figure 6.2 Wage ladder.

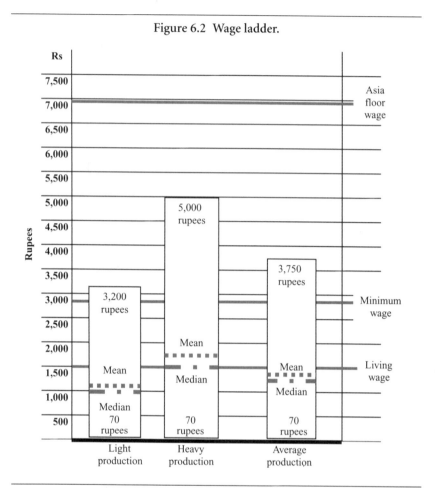

Perceived Fair Pay

Although tailors and embroiderers differed in the wages they earned and the extent that they received living wages because of the numbers of artisans in each category receiving work, most artisans felt similarly about the fairness of their pay. Of the artisans who were asked whether the pay they received for their work was fair, 80 percent agreed that it was. While pay was considered fair, it was still common for artisans to indicate that they would like to be able to earn more, by working more steadily throughout the year. One woman lamented,

> But there is not enough work. I feel the amount per piece is fair, but when orders are light and the income goes down, it is not enough.

However, some artisans who were dissatisfied with the pay linked their sentiments with the failure to earn what was perceived to be a living wage. For example, one artisan explained that she "has to run the house" and she does not earn a sufficient amount, elaborating that "she'd like to earn twenty to twenty-five rupees more per piece." Another explained more simply that "it is not enough. It is very hard to live on the income."

Differences in Economic Livelihood by Group

Artisan wages varied significantly between the seven workshops. The most successful workshops were Arpan, Sahara, and Ghar Udyog, whose artisans earned average wages from 1,600 to 1,956 rupees. Next in terms of wages earned were the groups WARE (Women Artisans Rehabilitation Enterprise) and Pushpanjali that earned from 1,232 to 1,377 rupees on average. Both WARE and Pushpanjali earned significantly less than Ghar Udyog, Arpan, and Sahara and significantly more than Udan Mandal and Ashiana. These latter two groups earned only 967 to 1,004 rupees on average.[14]

The outcomes of having differing wage levels between the groups vary. Interestingly, there was no significant difference between the artisans associated with the various groups in the ability of their households to meet Basic Minimum Needs (see Figure 6.3). Despite the widely disparate wages between groups, on average, artisans in each group are able to put together, with their additional household members, enough income to satisfy their households' minimum needs. However, the groups' abilities to provide artisans with living wages differ significantly (see Table 6.2). The groups with

Figure 6.3 Basic Minimum Needs ratio for artisans by group.

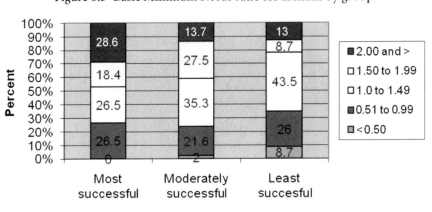

Table 6.2 Percentage of each group earning living wage or higher

GROUP	PERCENTAGE EARNING LIVING WAGE OR HIGHER
Arpan	76
Sahara	75
Ghar Udyog	56
WARE (Women Artisans Rehabilitation Enterprise)	41
Pushpanjali	30
Ashiana	25
Udan Mandal	14

the greatest proportion of artisans receiving living wages of 1,350 rupees or more work with Arpan, Sahara, and Ghar Udyog. In contrast, Udan Mandal provides living wages for only 14 percent of its artisans and Ashiana and Pushpanjali provide living wages to only 25 percent and 30 percent of their artisans, respectively. WARE provides living wages to just four out of ten of its artisans. We suspect that the groups are highly attuned to the needs of their members and that the ability of many households in every group to cover the basic needs is not accidental. Decisions on the size of the groups and work distributions likely take into account the needs of artisans' families rather than the needs of individual artisans that would be reflected in the living wage.

Artisan Characteristics Related to Economic Success

Do individual characteristics lead artisans working with Arpan, Sahara, and Ghar Udyog to consistently outearn their peers who work with other groups? Worker characteristics including age, education, and the number of children were not different for groups with differing levels of success. In addition, experience at previous jobs did not differ across the three success levels.[15] However, marital status differed between the three groups. The least successful groups (Udan Mandal and Ashiana) tended to have more heavy representation of women who were widowed or had been abandoned by their husbands (24.2 percent) and lower representation of never married artisans (3.0 percent) as compared with most successful groups (15.7 percent widowed/abandoned, 12.5 percent never married) and moderately successful groups (9.7 percent widowed/abandoned, 9.7 percent never married)[16]. The least successful group had more artisans who had sole responsibility for their economic livelihood. Reflecting on the earnings differences among artisans, Pushpika comments that

> often times over the years we have seen that many women who are capable are also the leaders and the ones who will make whatever happen to survive and thrive. And then there are women who do not have the leadership qualities who definitely have the need. Because not everyone is a leader, not everyone is able to make the most of the opportunities.

Cultural expectations about appropriate work for women led us to also examine how the gender composition of the groups was related to earnings. Groups composed of all women or a mix of men and women earned similar wages both on average or when work was slow; however, the mixed gender groups earned significantly higher wages than the all female groups when work was heavy.[17] This is easily explained since the mixed groups, which have long histories with MarketPlace, tend to receive a larger number of orders with quick deadlines because they have established their reliability for meeting these high-pressure deadlines. The differences among the groups in their artisans' ability to earn a living wage and the relationships between gender composition and wages warrant examination by MarketPlace to understand whether there are lessons about leadership, productivity, or other practices that can be learned from the most successful groups and shared with those in the less successful groups.

Conclusions

In this chapter, we have examined the economic livelihood gained by artisans working with MarketPlace: Handwork of India. Without question, the artisans and their household members described here are better off than if they did not have the work that MarketPlace provides; despite that many are likely underemployed. Underemployment is most problematic for some of the neediest women artisans that MarketPlace seeks to empower—those who have been widowed, abandoned, or face a lifetime of abuse from their husbands or joint families. Most artisans reflect an eagerness to work longer hours and earn higher pay, as reflected by the jump in earnings associated with heavier production schedules. However, without greater demand for MarketPlace products and the associated rise in production levels, opportunities for the women remain limited. Recognizing that there is more to well-being than an artisan's economic situation, the next chapter examines the multiple dimensions of well-being and how MarketPlace contributes to a better quality of life.

Notes

1. The analysis in this chapter is based primarily on the following interview questions:

- Please describe the persons who live in your household and their ages. Record as son, daughter, husband, wife, mother-in-law, sister, brother, etc. What is the average monthly income for each person? For those indicating a range, record the minimum monthly salary and the maximum monthly salary.
- Does your household have any other sources of income? (Probe for any monthly rent from a subtenant.)
- Does your household have any other way to provide for your needs? (Probe for noncash contributions such as a family member who brings food or grains from their native place.) What are they?
- In a typical month, with an income of ___, how much money is typically spent for each of the following: housing, food, school expenses, transportation, fuel for cooking, doctor's visits/medicines, clothing/jewelry, entertainment, going to native place, loans, other?
- How often in a week do you come to the workshop? How long do you work when you are there (or stay for those who primarily work at home)? How many hours do you spend on your tailoring/embroidery at home? Also, how many days per week do you work? Additionally, the second group of artisans interviewed were asked about their weekly working hours as follows: During times when orders are heavy? During times when orders are light?

2. SD = 701. Exchange rate at the time of data collection was 48 rupees to US$1. Analysis of variance revealed that tailors averaged significantly higher wages than embroiderers during both heavy, $F(1,147) = 11.01$, $p = .001$, and light, $F(1,147) = 9.29$, $p = .003$, work times, and when incomes were averaged across the fluctuating production levels, $F(1,147) = 13.08$, $p = .000$.

3. SD = 0.9

4. SD = 1,597

5. One household had two sons receiving high monthly incomes working as assistants in Bollywood.

6. We gathered estimates of monthly expenditures on food, housing, utilities, entertainment, and personal loans (see Table 6.3). A small number of missing values for housing, food, transportation, and utilities were replaced by the average. For expenditures that occurred irregularly throughout the year, such as medical costs, transportation to visit family, and clothing, we asked artisans to provide an estimate of annual expenses. To identify the fairly varied expenditures households

Table 6.3 Household expenditures and Basic Minimum Needs (in rupees)

	MEAN	SD
Basic Monthly Expenditures		
Housing	258	439
Food	2,168	1,112
Transportation	142	223
Water	71	82
Cooking fuel	237	102
Electricity	269	218
Entertainment	57	121
Non-mortgage loans	331	746
Annual Expenditures		
Medical	2,110	3,042
Clothing	1,787	2,007
Travel home or other destination	1,421	1,997
Household Basic Minimum Needs (housing, food, transportation, and utilities)	3,145	1,308

had on fees for school attendance, we asked for estimated annual expenditures from the first group of artisans interviewed, had the second group of artisans estimate their monthly expenditures, and then calculated an average monthly amount using the combined data. This was done in efforts to ensure that estimates of school expenditures were accurate; however, expenditures among the artisans were so widely varied, estimates like averages become of somewhat less value.

7. Expenditures on food and household size had a weak, but significant correlation ($r = .257$, $p = .001$).

8. SD $= 1,308$

9. $n = 33$

10. We first conducted multiple regression using scores on the Basic Minimum Needs ratio as the dependent variable and type of job and amount of work time (days per week at both the home and workshop and hours per day at both the home and workshop) as independent variables. The models were not significant. Whether the artisan served as a tailor or embroiderer did not make a difference, nor did the hours worked per day and days worked per week. A model regressing average artisan wages, average spouse wages, and average other wages was significant, $F(3,112) = 14.36$, $p = .000$, and had an R^2 of .278. Both average spouse wages ($b = .41$, $t = 5.00$, $p = .000$) and other wages ($b = .38$, $t = 4.59$, $p = .000$) were significant in predicting the Basic Minimum Needs ratio but average artisan salary was not a significant predictor.

11. We conducted discriminant analysis between the two groups. The discriminant function was significant (Wilks' lambda $= .889$, $p = .004$). Structure matrix

Table 6.4 Differences between pairs of artisan groups

	GHAR UDYOG	WARE (WOMEN ARTISANS REHABILITATION ENTERPRISE)	SAHARA	UDAN MANDAL	PUSHPANJALI	ARPAN	ASHIANA	F	p
Average artisan wages	1,600[abc]	1,377[de]	1,691[fgh]	1,004[adf]	1,232[bgi]	1,956[cijk]	967[chk]	6.37	.000
Minimum artisan wages	1,241[ab]	1,020[cd]	1,238[ef]	807[aegh]	1,152[gi]	1,438[chij]	520[bdfij]	4.13	.000
Maximum artisan wages	1,959[abc]	1,733[def]	2,144[ghi]	1,200[adgj]	1,311[behk]	2,474[cfijkl]	1,414[il]	7.00	.000

Note: Values in each row with the same superscript are significantly different.

loadings/standardized discriminant function coefficients for the independent variables were as follows: spouse wages (.781/.921), artisan wages (.373/.385), and others' wages (.303/.450). In cross-validation, 73.3 percent of cross-validated cases were grouped correctly with the discriminant function.

12. We calculated what scores on the Basic Minimum Needs ratio would be if only spouses and other household members, not the artisans, were earning. The average score was 0.93 and only 39.7 percent of households had scores of 1.0 or greater.

13. We conducted tests of difference on several variables to determine if those earning the living wage (maximum salary earned by artisan was 1,350 rupees or more) had differing patterns of work or personal characteristics than those who did not earn the living wage (maximum salary less than 1,350 rupees). There were no significant differences in the length of employment with MarketPlace ($F(1,108) = 0.354$, $p = .553$), number of days worked in the workshop ($F(1,111) = 0.349$, $p = .556$) or at home ($F(1,107) = 0.711$, $p = .401$), number of hours worked at home ($F(1,109) = 0.215$, $p = .614$), hours worked in the workshop ($F(1,107) = 0.579$, $p = .449$), or levels of educational attainment ($F(1,122) = 0.235$, $p = .629$). Chi-square analysis showed that those earning the living wage tended to be tailors rather than embroiderers ($\chi^2(1,90) = 6.37$, $p = .013$).

14. Table 6.4 shows significant differences between pairs of artisan groups.

15. Analysis of variance was used to test if three groups (most successful:Arpan, Sahara, and Ghar Udyog, moderately successful:WARE and Pushpanjali, and least successful:Ashiana and Udan Mandal) significantly differed in the age of their artisan workers, $F(2,145) = 0.75$, $p = .472$, education, $F(2,156) = 1.17$, $p = .312$, and artisans' number of children, $F(2,136) = 0.71$, $p = .493$. Chi-square analysis compared distribution of artisans holding previous jobs by the three groups, $\chi^2 = 2.84$, $p = .242$. Significantly different by success of group was the number of hours/day worked at home, $F(2,139) = 3.92$, $p = .22$; the most successful groups worked 6.4 hours daily, moderately successful groups worked 5.3 hours daily, and least successful groups worked 4.9 hours per day at home. In addition, there was a significant difference between groups on the number of hours per day they worked

Table 6.5 Maximum wages for mixed-gender and all-female groups (in rupees)

	MEAN (SD) FOR MIXED-GENDER GROUPS	MEAN (SD) FOR ALL-FEMALE GROUPS	F
Average artisan wages	1,524 (562)	1,323 (780)	3.37
Minimum artisan wages	1,146 (621)	1,052 (655)	0.84
Maximum artisan wages	1,902 (663)	1,594 (1,060)	4.66*

*$p < .05$.

at the workshop, $F(2,137) = 4.16$, $p = .018$; most successful 3.1, moderate 4.0, least 5.0 hours per day at the workshop.

16. Whether distribution of marital status was significantly different by differing levels of groups' success was tested with chi-square ($\chi^2 = 13.86$, $p = .031$).

17. Analysis of variance indicated significantly different maximum wages for mixed-gender and all-female groups (see Table 6.5).

CHAPTER 7

Well-Being

I never thought I would work and make my own living. I have learned so much. Otherwise I would be under someone else's influence. Now I am free.

I have an identity of my own now.

I realize the importance of knowing myself so that I can love myself. If I do not love myself, how can I expect others to love me?

Robert Chambers' model of development identifies multiple dimensions of well-being, including material, psychological, social, and spiritual. After considering the artisans' general level of well-being, this chapter focuses on Chambers' first three dimensions.[1] Material well-being encompasses changes women have made in their housing, diets, and health care, and identifies consumer products purchased for the household. Psychological well-being speaks to the women's self-respect, confidence, and courage. Finally, social well-being addresses social interactions among women in the workshops as well as in their homes. As women gain confidence, they begin to make decisions within the household that were formerly left to other family members. Respect for the artisan is transformed within the family and among neighbors. The chapter ends with discussion of social action projects undertaken by MarketPlace groups. Through these projects, artisans reach out to their communities by contributing to well-being within a larger context. Projects contribute to improved sanitation, health, and foodstuffs, and to expanded knowledge about women's rights. These innovative programs provide value-added opportunities for individual and community development in conjunction with MarketPlace income generation.

General Well-Being

Considering how artisans perceive their well-being at a general level provided a starting point for considering the extent and means that well-being is enhanced through work with Marketplace. We used a global assessment of satisfaction with life to understand how artisans perceive their well-being. As they reflected on their satisfaction with life prior to beginning work with MarketPlace, artisans rated satisfaction as having been an average of 2.3 on a seven-point scale. In comparison, since coming to work with MarketPlace, artisans rated their satisfaction with life as a 5.7 on the same scale, a statistical increase of 3.4 points from the pre-Marketplace rating.[2] Artisans clearly believe that their well-being has been enhanced as a result of their work. An artisan compares the changes in her life after joining MarketPlace with the experiences of many other Indian women.

> In the villages, a woman is not given the freedom to do anything, because if she steps out of the house unmarried, people throw aspersions on her. I came to live in the city of Mumbai after marriage along with my husband. He was not able to earn enough money there. I decided to look for work. I felt shy but I gathered my strength and stepped out of the house looking for work and my life has become better since then. Earlier my husband would scold me saying if you cannot live on the money I bring home then go back to the village—you don't have to run here and there for work. But I did not listen to him because I wanted at least some comforts in my home. That is why I took up working at Sahara. I am the mother of two children and am living happily with them now.

Material Well-Being

Material well-being is the enhanced quality of life that comes from expanded ability to provide for personal and household needs. Material well-being is supported by a steady flow of income to meet daily needs for living. Knowing that artisans had much greater satisfaction with life since beginning their work with MarketPlace, it seemed that the higher levels of satisfaction would be based on monetary indicators. Yet, there was no connection between the artisans' actual wages or total household income and their satisfaction with life. Higher personal and household incomes did not lead to increased satisfaction with life nor did lower personal and household incomes contribute to diminished satisfaction with life.[3] With this finding, we speculated that psychological and social dimensions of well-being were having a much stronger impact than material well-being on overall feelings of well-being; however, we wanted to further investigate how artisans felt about their ability to provide for their families' needs. When comparing artisans' perceived abilities to provide for their families both before ($M = 2.0$) and after coming to work with MarketPlace ($M = 5.4$), we found a marked improvement since the work commenced.[4] The dual findings of improved satisfaction with life and greater perceived ability to provide for their families' needs further support that work with MarketPlace has made a real contribution to these artisans' quality of life.

Like satisfaction with life, the monetary indicators of artisan and total household income did not show a direct link with perceived ability to provide for the family. Even the extent that Basic Minimum Needs were covered by the income incurred in the household was not related to perceived ability to provide for these needs.[5] These findings suggest that artisans perceive that their material well-being has been enhanced to a greater extent than it actually has. However, when artisans perceived that they were better able to provide for their families they did have higher ratings of satisfaction with life or overall well-being.[6] The more that an artisan felt she had provided for her family, the more likely she was to be satisfied with her life. These seemingly conflicting findings led us to further explore artisans' feelings of improved well-being from acquisition of material things.

We examined a variety of additional indicators of artisan material well-being, including general improvements in providing for the household, regularity of meals, ability to save money for special purposes, improvements to the home, education received by children, enhanced medical care, attention to appearance, and enhanced self-esteem and independence. Areas of expanded material well-being were discussed frequently by the artisans as they reflected on the most important changes they have experienced and observed in others as a result of their work with MarketPlace. Some artisans describe their general improved ability to provide for themselves and their families.

> My lifestyle has been improved greatly. Food, clothing, shelter . . . all the basic things I now have.

An important indicator of enhanced material well-being is the ability of the artisans to provide regular meals for themselves and their household members. Only two out of ten artisans reported that they or their children at times did not have enough to eat or had to skip a meal for financial reasons. For those who missed meals, most did so very infrequently, having too little to eat only one time per month.

Rather than missing meals, many artisans chose instead to borrow from relatives and neighbors during emergency situations. Comments made regarding missing meals expressed the priority put on feeding the children and the shame that was felt when the mother was unable to do so.

> I borrow money from the neighbors if necessary, I do not believe in missing meals.

> Some days when I have little food available, I just have a cup of tea in the morning and can go on all day like this … but the children use lots of energy, and they need some food, so then I must go and borrow money from others to buy some food for them.

Although most do not miss meals, many artisans maintain fairly simple diets with few extras. The greatest number of artisans described a typical day's menu as including bread and tea for breakfast, and bread, rice and a vegetable for lunch and dinner. On Sundays and special occasions fish, chicken, mutton, or a special vegetable dish was served. A small number of families seldom had any fish, chicken, mutton, or special vegetable dishes; however, a similar number reported eating these food items on a daily basis. Despite these variations in quantity and variety appropriate to the artisans' religions, comments from artisans reflect an improved ability to feed both themselves and their families. Describing one of the things that she is most proud of, one artisan explained, "I can provide food for my family and I can get my own meal every day."

The opening of bank accounts and the ability to save money is an important indicator of material well-being as well, because it reveals the availability of some discretionary money that can be put aside for future needs. Four out of ten artisans report that they are able to save money from their paychecks, but only one-fourth of those asked are able to set aside money from every paycheck. For those who are able to save, money is being set aside for such things as their daughters' dowries and for the emergencies that might arise including irregular pay. As one artisan explained, "I need to save for when there is no work, so we can survive."

Having discretionary income means that many homeowners are able to make repairs or improvements on their homes. When noting important changes members of her group achieved as a result of working with MarketPlace, one artisan reported that "when people first join, their homes are not in good condition and they are able to make improvements." Nearly half of the artisans owning their homes reported they had made repairs or improvements to their homes as a result of the work with MarketPlace. The most common improvement was to add a second floor that would provide greater amounts of space for a large family or rental income in the slum where housing is at a premium. Other improvements included making renovations or improvements increasing the permanency of the home, such as tiling floors and walls, creating brick walls, and adding concrete rooves. As one artisan reported, "Before working at MarketPlace, our house was *kuccha*—made from cow dung and bricks; we have changed it to a *pukka* house with concrete walls." A few artisans reported adding utilities such as water taps, water tanks, electricity, and additional lighting.

Both renters and homeowners are able to buy consumer products to furnish their home when income exceeds that needed to cover basic expenditures. Just more than 57 percent of artisans indicated that they had purchased home furnishings or equipment for the home from their wages. The most frequently purchased item was a television. As one artisan explained, "I enjoy being able to do some of my work and watch television at the same time." Other new furnishings included gas cookers and cooking vessels, dishes and cooking utensils, and furniture items such as cupboards, chairs, beds, and wardrobes. Summing up the changes that can be made in one's home and home furnishings as a result of working with MarketPlace, one artisan explained, "Before MarketPlace, I lived in one room. Since MarketPlace, we bought our house and built another floor. We bought a water tank and electric lights."

Educating children is prioritized almost as highly as the most basic food and housing needs and their extensive enrollment in school reflects the artisans' expanded material well-being. The total number of children the artisans had was 418. Through inventories of household members and their occupation or school status, we found that a total of eighteen children under the age of eighteen were not attending school. Nine seventeen-year-old children had completed their schooling and worked; one additional child of age seventeen had finished school but did not work. One sixteen-year-old and four fifteen-year-old children were reported as being finished with school but not working. Some of those who were no longer attending school had completed their education at the eighth standard while a few others had failed out of school at higher levels. Finally, three children were described as being handicapped and unable to attend school because of the high expense of special education. With these few exceptions, all of the artisans' children under the age of eighteen were attending school. The ability to keep children enrolled in school, an indicator of enhanced material well-being, was described by several artisans as one of the most important changes in their lives as a result of working with MarketPlace.

I am sending the children to English Medium School. I never think of anything else but my children. My dream is that they have good jobs.

I have three children and I am helping them make their dreams come true. I don't mind about taking loans or that I am less educated, as long as the children get a good education.

My husband does a lot of gambling so I do not always get a lot of money from him. Now I can pay the school fees properly and on time.

Now I can pay for my children's education and I don't have to fear for their future.

Divergent opinions emerged about whether artisans take better care of their health now that they are with MarketPlace. Of the artisans asked, 69 percent of artisans reported taking better care to maintain their health, acknowledging that if they are not healthy they cannot do their work.[7] However, if the health need was more expensive such as an x-ray, they would think carefully how the cost of the x-ray would affect their children and their family's ability to eat. Devi Nair, a MarketPlace social worker, noted that Hindu women fast for many ritual reasons such as offering a blessing for a husband or giving thanks for a wish coming true. Devi, a Hindu herself, has tried to point out that the women need to retain their strength to care for their families and complete the MarketPlace work. She has urged balance in attending to health and spiritual needs.

MarketPlace social workers and artisans also observe that as women's income has increased, their appearance has changed. As one artisan explained,

> The clothing of the women has changed because they can better afford it now. Fashion only follows when health and food are well taken care of.

Women no longer are limited to wearing old, torn saris. As one artisan elaborated,

> When I used to only make 200 rupees a month I used to just think and dream about buying dresses and clothes. Now I buy clothes for all of the family.

Manesha, the proprietor of Pushpanjali, asks that the women come to the workshop "dressed nicely with proper earrings and matching bangles." She treats coming to the workshop like coming to a job and the women are expected to look nice.

Beyond the many material things that money can buy, earning money also imparts well-being by improving self-confidence, enhancing artisan independence, and fostering respect from others in the household. One artisan reflected on changes she had seen in others,

> The women have money in their own hands now and they do not have to depend on their husbands for money.

In summary, investigation of material well-being experienced by artisans who work with MarketPlace shows that while artisan income reflected underemployment and a somewhat inconsistent influence on actual ability to pay for household needs, many artisans have earned discretionary income that is invested in a variety of ways. Artisans strongly feel that their lives have improved materially. How have these artisans improved their psychological health and social relationships as a result of this work?

Psychological Well-Being

Artisans' simple answers of, "I can talk about anything here" or "I feel peaceful here" speak to the relief from tension and worry the women feel when at the workshops. Repeatedly, women shared their prior loneliness and isolation: "I had no one to talk with before I came here." Among these women, the workshops provide a critically important psychological refuge where "caste and religion do not matter" and where women can concentrate on their work away from household tensions. Over time, women come to realize that their problems are other women's problems as well. As they talk together, women acquire a sense of freedom and courage to make their own decisions. Women elaborate,

> When I am disheartened, I can share the problems with the women and get some ideas how to solve them. I like that part best.

> I used to be scared to go out of the house, now I feel OK. Now I can speak confidently, even to you [Earthwatch interviewer]!

> We have so many problems, but now that I am working my whole concentration is on my work so I don't think of my problems so much. In the past I thought of it all the time and I grew very thin.

Freedom from worry and fear evolves over time into general expressions of happiness to be among newfound friends. Artisans commented,

> I am much happier now. I never imagined that my house would be so good. Other family members are also very happy.

> I never thought I would have so many friends.

> If I am feeling anxious, I can go to [name of workshop] and relax with my friends.

> I like that we make each other laugh and think, play word games, tell jokes, and our tensions go away.

One woman even shared that when she doesn't go to the workshop for one or two days, the other women search her out. They miss her as she has become quite effective in helping people laugh and release their tensions.

Women who previously rarely left their homes talk about how "scared" they were to do anything on their own. Widows talked of the fright they felt when they realized they were now responsible for their children. Insecurities due to a dark complexion, disfigurements from leprosy, lack of formal education, and inexperience in speaking in public surfaced. However, the group members assist each other in overcoming their fears and garnering self-respect.

> I have learned to struggle with life, like I have some power . . . I don't feel so powerless. There is inspiration that I can change some things in my life.

> I was unaware of how to speak in front of people and even how to have conversations because I had always lived in a village. Now I know how to meet and talk with other people.

> I used to not attend meetings or even have contact with other people. Now I will join protest groups!

Acknowledging the emotional support they received at the workshops, the artisans generously expressed concern for other non-MarketPlace women who have no one with whom to talk. One artisan told of a neighbor who during the previous week set fire to herself and "expired." The artisan believed that had her neighbor been part of the group, the members could have talked with her about her problems and helped her to understand that burning is self-centered and "thinking only of yourself." Together, the group members pondered what would happen to the woman's three young children.

As women's strength and confidence emerges, they start to alter their views about what women can accomplish in their lives. As one artisan stated, "I have learned many things, the most important of which is to dream and to realize my dreams." Several women elaborated:

> I used to think girls shouldn't leave the home. Now I think all girls should go out and work. As I started going out myself, I felt better. I could share my joys and sorrows. This is my first time to have friends. I have started traveling on my own and telling my opinions to others. I want to go forward.

> I have come to realize my inner potential. I was always a person who wanted to work hard but I was not confident. The people around you [say] you should not go out because there are ghosts or you will be attacked. What they really want is to keep you weak and at home.

I know that I can do a lot. I know that I have a lot of potential. I do my MarketPlace work and also take full charge of the house as my mother is ill. Before people would ask me, "Why don't you get a husband?" Now I don't feel that I need one.

Social Well-Being

Social well-being was often explained in terms of meaningful friendships the women developed with their coworkers. Artisans also value the knowledge they have gained to assist them in interacting with other women and with the often challenging social dynamics of their households. Several women explained.

> At [name of group], the women all share their problems at home and I can speak to them about how to solve them.

> I had few friends before, and now I have gained a lot of knowledge from making these new friends.

> I learn various things regarding behavior of children, how to deal with my mother-in-law, how to get along with my husband. These are skills I didn't know before coming here.

> My husband used to hit and shout at me a great deal before I was working. Now he doesn't beat me but still shouts at me about going out or not dressing nicely. He has started realizing about women's rights and law since I am telling him from what I have learned.

One woman even suggested that her husband, who used to criticize her for wanting to talk with the other women in the neighborhood, has started to understand the importance to her of socializing with her friends.

The metaphor of family surfaces repeatedly in the women's discussions of their workshops.

> We are like a small family, not mine, not yours, everyone's. If need be, we make visits to our homes to help each other.

> [Name of workshop] is like a mother to us. It shelters us and cares for us. One of the women's husbands used to go out drinking. He never used to work and he threw her and their daughters out of the house, so they were living at my house. We all came together in a meeting about this and went to her husband and talked to him and got him to realize what he had done and he went into treatment and got better.

Women not only conceptualized their workshops as family but also used their earnings to further strengthen their own family bonds. One woman expressed pride that she now had the money to pay for public transportation so she could travel across Mumbai to visit her married daughter on a regular basis. Another woman saved rupees to buy her brother a cupboard that was presented at the opening ceremony for his new house. Still another remarked about being able to fix up her mother's house and to buy her new things, all of which she never would have dreamed she could do.

One woman, when talking about family, noted that by working at home she was able to curb some emerging problems with her teenaged son. Earlier when she was part of another MarketPlace workshop where she sewed at the workshop premises, she felt she was spending too much time at the workshop and neglecting her children. Her son was under the influence of some bad peers and not studying. Now that she has transferred to a second MarketPlace workshop closer to her home, she is able to work more hours at home. She assesses that the flexibility that MarketPlace offers in integrating work and family responsibilities has enhanced her family well-being.

Not only do women cement bonds with their colleagues and family, but they also become curious about social life beyond the slums.

> I get information about the outside world now. I used to just be at home and now I am more curious about the world, what is going on around me and in other countries, other parts of India. It has increased my curiosity. I understand more about people, why they are like they are.

Household Respect and Decisions

As part of the interviews, artisans were asked directly about the decisions they made within the household and whether their work with MarketPlace translated into increased respect from family and friends. Women believed that their work parlayed into enhanced respect across all household members, with an increase in respect of 70 percent from husbands and 63 percent from in-laws. Among children, 88 percent offered greater regard for their mothers. Respect permeated to the women's neighborhoods as well with 83 percent of the women experiencing greater esteem from others living nearby.

Artisans were also queried about involvement of themselves and family members (husband, children, in-laws) in decision making. As shown in Table 7.1, MarketPlace women currently make a number of household-related decisions either solely or jointly with their husbands. While we have no comparative data to which we can contrast the artisans' current decision making with their past influence, we suspect that the women's impact may

Table 7.1 Decision making in the household (percentages)

TYPE OF DECISION	WOMAN	MAN	SHARED	IN-LAWS	CHILD
School son/daughter attends	43.5	19.6	37.0		
Number of children	32.1	19.0	44.0	1.2	
Daughter's job/activities	32.8	19.7	31.1	1.6	14.8
Son's job/activities	26.8	15.5	33.8	1.4	22.5
Daughter's marriage age	22.7	16.9	45.8	8.4	1.2
Choice of husband for daughter	22.4	22.4	38.2	6.6	10.5

have increased substantially over time. Interestingly, across all categories of household decisions, in-laws have limited influence in the final decision; in all cases the percentages are below 10 percent.

In examining specific categories of decision, 80 percent of the artisans choose either singly or jointly with their husbands the schools that their sons and daughters attend. An even higher percentage (85 percent) regularly attend meetings with teachers at their children's schools. They use these meetings to monitor their children's progress and to ask questions of the teachers so they can better help their children succeed in school. One artisan disclosed that when her husband was alive, he used to go to the children's school to sign forms and annual reports. When he died, she had to go in his place. She didn't know how to sign her name and was both scared and embarrassed. They took a stamp with her thumb. Although she was initially very nervous with a pen in her hand, she practiced in Urdu, Hindi, and English. Now she is not afraid to use a pen at any time and regularly attends school meetings. Another artisan adds additional evidence of the impact she has on her children's education.

> Now I can persuade my husband that my daughters should continue to study and not get married before they are ready. My eldest daughter wanted to go to college but my in-laws and my husband [persuaded by the in-laws] said that she must leave education and get married. I stood my ground and managed to persuade my husband to let our daughter go to college. Because of my work with [name of workshop], I have enough income for my daughter to go. Now I feel I can persuade my husband to let all of our daughters continue their studies as long as they wish.

Women are also significantly involved in decisions as to the number of children they will bear (76 percent) and in decisions that impact their children's choice of jobs, activities, and attitudes (65 percent for daughters,

61 percent for sons) (see Table 7.1). Casual conversations in which women repeatedly voiced the wish that they and their daughters would have greater input into the daughters' marriages is borne out in the interview data. Of women whose daughters had already married or were soon to marry, the women reported that 70 percent of the daughters had a say in the choice of their husbands; for the majority of daughters, this involved responding to a potential mate put forward by the girls' parents or a combination of the parents and fathers' family. One woman describes the marriage negotiations for her daughter.

> When my daughter was sixteen years old she began a job, and also studied computers. When she was twenty, she "met" a boy in Bangalore through the internet. When they decided to get married, I told his family that my husband had left me and I had worked very hard to bring up my two children myself. I wanted them to know the truth. I am very proud that my daughter found her own husband. Between her earnings and mine, we paid for her wedding. I did not pay any dowry. I am proud of my daughter. She is educated and her husband knows that what she brings to her family are her accomplishments and values—which are more valuable than any dowry.

However, when a daughter's marriage did not go as planned, then another mother stepped in to assist.

> My second daughter got married and her in-laws used to pour hot tea on her arm and burn her. I told her to divorce her husband. We went to court and now she is divorced and runs her own beauty parlor.

Increased respect garnered from family members provides additional evidence of enhanced social well-being associated with MarketPlace work. Of particular note is the significant increase in respect artisans received from their children (88 percent) and neighbors (83 percent). Repeatedly, artisans relayed that their children were very proud of their mothers' work with MarketPlace. Several women expressed with pride how their sons sought them out for advice (an uncommon occurrence in India's male-dominated society), helped with housework, and made them tea when they returned home very tired after a long day at a MarketPlace workshop. Children liked that their mother participated in their schools. In several cases, women assessed that their own hard work acted as an incentive for their children to "try their best with their studies." In the Global Dialogue sections of several recent MarketPlace catalogs, daughters voice their feelings for their mothers.

My mother's involvement in MarketPlace has changed my life. Earlier, my mother would not let me step out of the house, but after she got associated with MarketPlace, she started encouraging me to be independent and supported me in school. I am a very confident person and an optimist.

I want to complete my graduation and start my own small business. I am proud of being the daughter of [name]. She is uneducated but she has always encouraged me to study. She has fought against all odds to educate me. I know that my mother is working with an organization where everyone is treated equally, and everyone gets an opportunity to grow.

Neighbors also offer positive remarks to the artisans; for Muslim women, an all-woman group is respected.

I am thought of as a good example for other women. I am well respected because although I am sick and my husband is absent, I do all my MarketPlace work and my house work. My neighbors say to their daughter-in-laws, "Why can't you be more like [name]?"

My neighbors respect me. I work to support my family and yet my work does not involve seeing men. They also like that the work is flexible enough for me to take time off to take care of relatives who come to stay.

People look at me with different eyes now that I am working every day. People who are working everyday with all women get more respect. There should be more workshops with all women in them. It is particularly good for widows but really good for all women.

One community conveyed their respect for the leader of one of the MarketPlace groups when she was asked to hoist the Indian national flag in her community on August 15, an event held each year to commemorate India's independence from British rule. The artisan describes her pride.

I was scared and nervous and was feeling very odd that I, being a woman, was hoisting the flag where my husband and other men were standing as an audience. I think that at that time my husband also might have felt a little jealous. But the decision about me hoisting the flag was taken by the members living in my community and I was officially sent a letter requesting me to do so. While I was hoisting the flag I felt so proud and thought to myself why am I feeling scared? I am doing something to be proud of and being a woman I do not need to be behind in anything.

Increased respect also emerged from husbands and in-laws.

> My husband treats me better. He has given me more independence than before. [He] never used to let me go out of house before I started working with MarketPlace.

> When we still lived with my in-laws, my husband didn't pay much attention to me. He didn't give me much care or protection from them, I had a difficult life there. But after he became sick and they threw us out, and after I built our house and cared for him until he was well all while providing for our family, he very much respected me.

Several cited fewer quarrels with their husbands once they were earning; however, pride was not always expressed directly to the artisan. While several women have convinced their husbands to quit drinking, others wonder whether their husbands may actually drink more.

> My husband thinks he is the main person in the family so what I do doesn't matter. He never says good things to me directly but brags to his parents and they are impressed with what I do.

> He encourages me to go to work. He especially respected me when I was the only earner and he was sacked from his job for absenteeism. He was later given his job back. Sometimes however, he is suspicious of me going out. I think perhaps that he drank more at one time because I was sharing responsibility for earning more money.

Some husbands' friends continue trying to convince them that their wives are doing the wrong thing working. They say the wives should be at home caring for their husbands and the houses.

SHARE Signature Programs: Social Action and Global Dialogue

In the first part of this chapter, we focused on evidence of well-being from individual artisan's perspectives. In this section, we describe SHARE (Support the Handicapped's Rehabilitation Effort) programs whereby women work together to improve their lives, broaden their outlook on the world, and make important contributions in their communities. These programs highlight MarketPlace's integrated model of business and development that attend closely to women's lives both inside the workshops and beyond. Initially, that larger world encompasses their neighborhoods and other women of Mumbai. To this end, each MarketPlace artisan group has taken on a social action project that engages them in their communities. Projects have addressed community issues such as sanitation, food rations, and health care.

Disgusted with the terrible sanitation conditions in their slum, the twenty-eight members of Pushpanjali initiated a two-step program for cleaning up the alleys and pathways near their homes. First, women went from door to door asking their neighbors to halt the common practice of throwing garbage directly outside their doorways. The artisans provided information to their neighbors about the health advantages for depositing refuse in trash containers. During the second step, Pushpanjali artisans delivered demands to municipal authorities that their trash be picked up regularly and that sewage drains be sprayed and covered.

Energized by the success of their first social action project, the artisans next joined women from other slums at morchas (rallies) in calling for governmental overhaul of the corrupt rationing system. Initially, the ration system was created in India to provide basic necessities such as rice and wheat at a subsidized price to low-income populations. However, over time the governmental system became riddled with corruption in multiple ways. Foodstuffs are often adulterated and unavailable to those citizens most in need. Women must stand in line for hours to receive their allotments. A MarketPlace staff person describes the women's experiences as rally participants against corruption.

> The MarketPlace network group joined hands with 150 voluntary agencies and over 10,000 people convened at Govandi, one of the largest slums in Mumbai. The aim of this demonstration was to start a dialogue with politicians and political parties, to pressure them to make this issue a priority in their election campaign and to find out where they stood on this issue. This experience left the women with the knowledge that they were part of a larger movement. More concretely, these women have been able to control the quality of rations, prevent black-marketing of stock in two shops, and they had authorities seize a stockpile of grain worth 25,000 rupees being illegally hoarded and sold in one ration shop. During this process, the women tasted power in a situation that had previously left them feeling powerless and frustrated. They realized that they could actually make people accountable, even people more educated, richer, and more influential than they are.

In a second artisan group, the members of WARE focused their social action on health issues for women and children. The WARE members first sought health care training offered through a social service agency in

Mumbai. Younger WARE members describe that while they took notes during the classes, the older illiterate women could only listen. Yet, when it came time for the final exam, the older women integrated what they had heard with their life experiences to surpass the younger members' scores with flying colors. With training completed, members divided into seven groups with names such as the Capsules, Vitamins, Injections, and Surgeons. Equipped with a set of simple hand-drawn posters, essential for teaching illiterate people, WARE teams regularly visit the other MarketPlace groups to educate on health issues such as the importance of teaching children not to eat dirt, taking the prescribed dosage of medicine rather than the common practice of overmedicating, and attending to fevered children as a warning that something is wrong. With initial training complete, the women have become a collaborative resource in assisting workshop members with health issues. Devi, the SHARE social worker, observes the women taking greater care of their own health; they go to the hospital for themselves, not just their children.

In addition to social action projects, each workshop sends two artisans to monthly meetings of the Global Dialogue project. In these meetings, artisans discuss and select themes for the next season's MarketPlace catalog. Once themes are identified, artisans contribute stories and photographs about daily life in India to share with the US customers. Catalog themes have included celebrating strong women, redefining community, transitions, celebrating our differences, the meaning of beauty, living in harmony with nature, the power of identity, debating dowry, and others.

Earlier catalogs often highlighted the challenges that women faced in apparel production. An artisan elaborates.

> During the monsoons in July, there was a week when there was knee deep water in our houses all the time. The electricity was cut off because of the danger of electric shocks and I had to sew and deliver six dresses the next day. If I did not, the entire business would not be able to deliver our order and that would cause problems with cash flow later. I was in such a state because I could not see enough to sew and the machine was half-way under water. Then my husband suggested that I put the machine on top of the bed—it was the only thing that was above water and my machine is a treadle machine, not electric. I had some broken candles so we put them in cooking vessels and floated them in the water. I got the six dresses done and gave them in the next day.

In contrast, more recent artisan stories tell about new opportunities for learning and recreation that have come about as the MarketPlace business evolved. A MarketPlace manager and an artisan, respectively, each describe a recent sports day.

> The artisans who have worked on these products have found freedom and economic independence through their work. This has enabled them to break away from oppressive traditions, enjoy life, and influence change. Recently their desire to learn new things took them out into the playing fields. While some had watched their children participate in school field events, many had never been to school themselves, and had never had the opportunity for physical education. Furthermore, married women are expected to be dignified and correct. So, the women artisans made their choice—to be undignified. They took the risk to look silly, to do something they had never done before, and to just plain have fun.

> The games were so good and made us feel that we have the right to enjoyment even at our age. Playing games is the best escape from our sorrowful thoughts and worries. When you win, the people around you clap and that makes you feel very happy and proud.

In addition to artisan-generated stories about their lives, artisans also frame questions in the catalog to which they solicit responses. In Evanston (US), a volunteer employee reviews the "global dialogue" letters and sends a summary of answers for discussion among the artisans in India. The Indian women have asked, "What are some of the family traditions that make you feel connected with your past? How is your household different than the one you were brought up in? What makes women decide or have the inner strength to get divorced?" On the other side of the globe, a US customer queried, "Does TV play a role in shaping the values of your children?" Another US customer's question, "What do you do in your free time?" led to intense discussion in India of what Americans mean by free time. For women who may walk several hours to collect water or take their children to school, the concept of free time was puzzling.

MarketPlace Work and Quality of Life

MarketPlace clearly espouses the 100% fair trade philosophy in its dual attention to income generation and to people-oriented development in its small, decentralized enterprises where attention to artisans as unique individuals is possible. At the outset of our research, we were guided by quality of life scholars, and interestingly by the artisans as well, to include a range of indicators for assessing artisans' lives and well-being. While MarketPlace artisans view their lives as significantly improved since joining MarketPlace, that improvement varies depending on how well-being is defined, whether it be from material, psychological, or social perspectives.

Although the artisans enumerated a number of tangible improvements in their diets, household repairs and furnishing, and children's schooling, their wages and household incomes did not statistically correlate with overall life satisfaction. In contrast, the psychological refuge of MarketPlace workshops has provided opportunities for women to talk with each other, gain solidarity, and emerge from abused or subservient positions in their households. With newfound confidence, artisans support each other in broadening their abilities to seek social justice for their children, families, and communities. For these artisans, life satisfaction seems closely linked to psychological and social well-being acquired in tandem with their incomes from MarketPlace. Each of the three dimensions of well-being, as defined by Chambers, provides a differing perspective on overall well-being or satisfaction. No one dimension alone provides a complete picture. Clearly, to these women, the benefits gained from their work went beyond the economic gain they provided to their families.

In 2005, the MarketPlace workshops were devastated by monsoon floods in Mumbai that wiped out much of their equipment and inventory. Pushpika Freitas uses a quality of life perspective when summarizing how the artisans and their workshops faced these new challenges.

> Three months have passed since the floods and on the surface things looked like they were pretty much back to normal. But looking deeper one could tell that the women had not completely recovered from the shock and losses they had experienced. The airing and sharing of their stories was helping them somehow to come to terms with all that had happened. It was during one of these discussions that I decided that it was time to go on a picnic, to give the women a chance simply to have fun and forget, at least for a day, all the responsibilities and worries that they face every single second of a normal day. MarketPlace has always prioritized recreation because the women always give this the lowest priority.
>
> So on October 22, 2005, we rented three huge buses to accommodate nearly 200 women and drove for two hours to Anand Resort. The recreation area consists of fifteen acres right on the beach, with a lot of trees and five swimming pools. After lunch the women were free to do whatever they wanted, and many of them split off to walk on the beach, sit on the swings, or chat in groups under the trees. To my astonishment, however, the biggest hit was the swimming pools. Since most of the women do not know how to swim (like me), and none

of them would ever in a million years be seen in a swimsuit, it hadn't occurred to me that the pools would be so popular. Yet after lunch more than half the women were in the pools, still wearing their saris and salwar-kurtas, scarves and all. They were splashing around, going on the water slides, singing and having the greatest time ever.

Looking back on the past twenty-five years, this day will be the highlight of my journey with MarketPlace. MarketPlace is not only about the economic benefits, the leadership building, the changes in family dynamics, and the participation of the women in family and community decisions. For me, it is about the overall quality of life. And life should include the opportunity to let your hair down (literally) and have fun, and the opportunity to bond with other women and share times like these. These are memories that will live forever for the women and me.

Notes

1. The analysis in this chapter is based primarily on the following interview questions. In addition, data are drawn from group meetings held by the authors with the artisans involved in social action projects.

a. What are some of the things you like most about being a part of [name of group]?

b. Overall, as you think about the past years that you have worked with [name of group], what have been the most important changes in your life?

c. As you have gained more skills at speaking out and providing for your family, are there any changes in your life that have been negative? Or have made life more difficult?

d. As you think about the other members of [name of workshop], what changes have you seen in the other members' lives as you look around you?

e. As you think about your life overall before you came to MarketPlace, how satisfied were you? (Answer on a seven-point scale with "1" = a sad face and "7" = a happy face.)

f. Now that you have been with MarketPlace, how satisfied are you with your life now? (Answer on a seven-point scale with "1" = a sad face and "7" = a happy face.)

g. Are you able to save any money?

h. Since working with MarketPlace, have you been able to make repairs or improvements in your home?

i. Have you been able to buy new furnishings, equipment?

j. Are there times when you or your children do not have enough to eat or have to skip a meal?
   • how often

k. Who takes the following decisions in your household?
- school that the daughter/son attends
- number of children you will have
- choice of daughter's career/job
- choice of son's career/job
- marriage age of daughter
- choice of husband for daughter

l. Do you feel that you receive more respect from any of the following people since you worked with [name of workshop]?
- husband
- in-laws
- children
- neighbors

2. We used seven-point Likert-type scales with pictorial endpoints (sad face vs. happy face) similar to a scale used by Brinkerhoff, Fredell, and Frideres (1997) for artisans to subjectively rate their general satisfaction with life both before working with MarketPlace and since working with MarketPlace. We also used the same scales to measure artisans' perceived ability to provide for their families' basic needs, both currently and before starting work with MarketPlace. A paired sample t-test comparing artisan ratings of satisfaction with life before coming to work for MarketPlace ($M = 2.32$, SD = 1.52) and after commencing work with MarketPlace ($M = 5.68$, SD = 1.32) showed a significant difference in the two ratings ($t = 20.77$, $p = .000$).

3. Table 7.2 presents the correlation analysis between various social indicators. There were no significant correlations between satisfaction with life and (a) artisan wages ($r = .107$, $p = .183$) or (b) total household income ($r = .063$, $p = .493$).

4. The paired sample t-test between artisans' ratings of their ability to provide for their family both before and after coming to work with MarketPlace was significant ($t = 21.99$, $p = .000$). SD (before) = 1.34, SD (after) = 1.42.

Table 7.2 Relationships between social indicators

SOCIAL INDICATOR	1	2	3	4	5	6
1. Artisan income	1.0					
2. Total household income	0.377*	1.0				
3. Basic expenses	0.165	0.617*	1.0			
4. Basic Minimum Needs ratio	0.325*	0.569*	−0.195	1.0		
5. Ability to provide basic needs	−0.085	0.002	−0.104	0.118	1.0	
6. Satisfaction with life	0.111	0.090	0.006	0.163	0.551*	1.0

*$p < .01$.

5. There were no significant correlations between perceived ability to provide for the family and (a) artisan wages ($r = .136, p = .090$) or (b) total household income ($r = .045, p = .620$) (see Table 7.1 earlier). In addition, there was no significant correlation between perceived ability to provide for the family and the score on the Basic Minimum Needs ratio ($r = -.114, p = .157$).

6. Satisfaction with life and perceived ability to provide for the family were moderately to highly correlated ($r = .604, p = .000$) (see Table 7.1).

7. To streamline the interviews, a few questions were asked of only artisans interviewed in the first two data collection sessions.

CHAPTER 8

Evaluation of Fair Trade Impacts, Certification and Viability of Artisan Work

I n *Artisans and Fair Trade: Crafting Development,* we offer our analysis of the everyday life of 161 textile artisans who have worked under a fair trade model that inextricably links economic and social goals. In response to those who have questioned artisan work as a pastime to fill empty hours or as an activity "unrelated to power and economic vitality" (Chatterjee 2007, 12; Wilkinson-Weber 1999), our MarketPlace: Handwork of India study portrays a markedly different picture. MarketPlace work offers a practical fit to the cultural context of the daily lives and household expectations for women living in Mumbai's slums. While for many women there is inadequate work to earn a living wage, particularly during seasons when orders are low, the wages are at the same time not inconsequential to the households involved. Large numbers of artisan households are able to pull together the income necessary to meet their basic needs and to provide some discretionary spending for household goods, home renovations, and other purchases. Beyond economic indicators, the women's story offers strong evidence of the "momentum that builds up in various corners of economic life" for application in realms well beyond the workplace (Guyer, Denzer, and Agbaje 2002, x). We turn now to MarketPlace's fair trade "ways of operating" (de Certeau 1984) for insights in answering the five sets of questions posed in Chapter 1 and from which we launched our analysis.

The Essence of MarketPlace and Its Fair Trade Model

In this section, we address our first set of questions on the MarketPlace model of fair trade: What principles and practices underlie the MarketPlace approach for integrating business and development? How does the Market-place approach fit the cultural context for artisans residing in the slums of Mumbai?

As MarketPlace grew and evolved, a tiny organization focused on making an economic contribution transformed to a much larger organization that provided dignified living conditions, opportunities for leadership development, and expanded social action and self-confidence for the 161 women we interviewed. Reflecting on the organization's impacts and how it differs from what others have accomplished in support of the poor through fair trade, Pushpika Freitas has identified five essential characteristics that define the essence of MarketPlace as a fair trade organization.

Grassroots Participation

Pushpika believes one of the most important elements of MarketPlace is its democratic processes and its insistence on 100 percent participation. The mission of the organization and its activities evolved one step at a time, in consultation with the artisans. As well, each producer group and the SHARE (Support the Handicapped's Rehabilitation Effort) social work staff makes certain that each artisan is engaged in some capacity building activity for leadership. The participation and leadership of artisans have influenced multiple processes, including even the meetings that Pushpika holds with the artisans when she is in Mumbai. Agendas for the meetings are planned by the groups and responsibility is delegated widely. Pushpika elaborates, "One of our saving graces is listening to the women and going at their pace. As opposed to having our own ideas about what should happen." By including artisans in the decision making of their work, SHARE and MarketPlace have encouraged the overall organization to evolve while maintaining sensitivity to each group's needs. As such, there are no strict rules of how groups organize and operate (e.g., this group must be a cooperative with thirty women). Each group's structure is different and is organized around the needs of its members.

Dual Focus on Income Generation and Social Programs

From the start, SHARE and MarketPlace focused on economics as a first step to empowerment. However, economic well-being has never been the sole focus of the work. Empowerment of disadvantaged women through leadership opportunities and social programs is at the core of their work as well. Integrating these dual foci has led to ownership by the women. Group members do whatever it takes to produce the garments, which ultimately contributes to capacity building. They learn and take notes about planning the cutting and production, using the telephone, procuring supplies outside the slum, and other tasks. In the process, the women hone leadership skills and increase their capacity to solve non-work–related problems. Groups have transferred these skills to their communities through social action projects.

Together, these opportunities propel the confidence of the women for further action and open doors for expanded opportunities and development.

Working in Groups

Not all women are entrepreneurs and not all situations lend themselves to individual entrepreneurship. In an Indian village, a woman might buy a cow and survive on the milk, but in Mumbai a woman cannot do that nor is it so easy to start selling vegetables or take up other income-producing activities as an individual. However, by working in groups, the women come together, combining their skills in support of each other. Furthermore, MarketPlace has created a platform where women feel free to talk about their problems and their needs. Group work and shared commitment have ignited the development programs and social systems that have evolved. The proximity in which the women live with each other in the slums has aided this process. While MarketPlace has set up work efficiently so that the women can collect their embroidery at the workshop and return home, the women often choose to remain in the workshop for a period of time—sitting together to relax, enjoying each other's company, and drawing on each other's strengths.

Groups Supporting Each Other

Beyond individual artisans working together to reach their production goals, a culture of intergroup reinforcement has also evolved. The supportive environment has been nurtured even though the groups compete with each other for orders. For example, the cutter for Ashiana traveled to her home village to visit her family, leaving the group in Mumbai unable to move forward with production. This dilemma was brought up at a production supervisors meeting and one of the leaders from Ghar Udyog volunteered to go and help the group with its cutting for several hours a day. The culture that has evolved between groups also guides the more established groups to take responsibility for the newer groups. For example, larger/older and smaller/newer groups are paired and check the accuracy of each other's fabric orders, as done by Ashiana and WARE. The groups share a belief that they are all in the effort together and often discuss how they might increase the number of groups.

Focus on Women in Family Context

Both Pushpika and the women affirm the centrality of the family unit in Indian life. However, through their education and development, the women are learning to subtly alter their formerly undervalued positions in the family and increase the support they receive from their husbands. For example, one woman in a Catholic/Hindu mixed marriage wanted to have her first child christened. She believed that religious training comes primarily from the mother when bringing up a child. The husband was against the baptism, but the wife reminded him that if the child was Catholic, he would be able to go to an English-speaking Catholic school. The husband did not have a job, which she did not hold over him; however, she subtly convinced him of the value of what she wanted to do. In another example of spousal support, a woman was engaged in a social action project and needed to go out in the evening to collect materials and make a poster. When she came home with the certificate for being involved in the project, her husband had it laminated and hung on the wall, thus clearly indicating to their children the mother's accomplishments and her status as a role model.

As we reflect on Pushpika's assessment, these essential characteristics of MarketPlace—grassroots participation, dual focus on income generation and social programs, working in groups, groups supporting each other, and the focus on women in family context—we note how they have synergistically worked to provide income, expand opportunities, and develop the capacities of the artisans involved. In a broad sense, MarketPlace offers a response to some of the conditions common to artisans throughout India (see Chapter 2)—conditions that preclude enterprise development and weigh heavily on the nation's social systems (see Table 8.1).

For the women at MarketPlace, the business approach provides an opportunity for work that fits the cultural context of their lives. Working at a job in a factory or as a domestic household employee for eight to ten continuous hours a day is not an option, given their responsibilities and commitments to caring for their children and households. As noted in Chapter 4, MarketPlace women do not follow a sequential pattern of compartmentalized activities across a day. Rather, childcare, household tasks, and MarketPlace work are interspersed throughout the day and take place in a relatively small geographic space of home and workshop. As John deGruchy, a Rockefeller Foundation scholar from South Africa, so aptly summarized following our presentation about MarketPlace at the Bellagio Center in Italy,

> You are studying a contextualized opportunity for women to work. Developing countries need diversity in work opportunities. It's not necessarily that one option, such as large factories or another option such as MarketPlace is better. It's not an either/or situation. Countries such as India need diversity in work opportunities to match the cultural contexts of different people's lives.

Table 8.1 MarketPlace response to conditions common among Indian artisans

COMMON CONDITION AMONG INDIAN ARTISANS	MARKETPLACE RESPONSE
Limited education	Opportunities offered for education related to reading, writing, health, child rearing, transportation, and women's rights. By working in groups, learning is shared and reinforced.
Limited exposure outside community or village	Global Dialogue expands awareness, as do trips to visit other workshops.
Cultural constraints (family, religion, gender) on acquiring capabilities	Workshops provide safe environment for women and individuals of varying religions to acquire capabilities related to work and for household and community application.
Resistance from family or community for women to travel for business reasons	Especially in all-female groups, women regularly travel, often in pairs, throughout Mumbai to deliver orders, acquire supplies, and visit other workshops
Little experience in expressing opinions	Decisions made in a democratic manner encourage women to express opinions. Women plan and lead workshop meetings.
Little experience in taking initiative	Community action projects encourage broad artisan involvement.
Limited time management skills beyond the household	Training offered in production planning (materials, time, costing) and in meeting orders in a timely manner.
Limited information about consumers of products	Global Dialogue fosters awareness of life beyond the slum and around the world.
Few income-producing opportunities	Workshops located in close proximity to artisans' homes and allowance for working in the home provide opportunities for employment without childcare, transportation, and other expenses.
Limited skills for employment	Apparel designs are adapted to fit the skills available for production; numerous workshops enhance skill levels.

MarketPlace Impact on Capabilities, Livelihood, and Well-Being of Women Textile Artisans

A second originating question addressed how MarketPlace, as a fair trade organization, impacted the lives of the women artisans who sewed and embroidered Indian-inspired apparel for the US market. Our discussion

Figure 8.1 MarketPlace pathway to capability acquisition, application, and transformation.

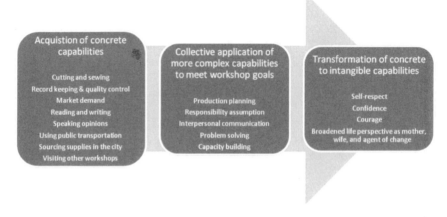

centers on changes in capabilities, livelihood, and well-being (Chambers 1997). How the MarketPlace approach to fair trade informs broader understanding on quality of life is also addressed.

Capabilities

The MarketPlace approach to work affords artisans with opportunities to acquire capabilities, apply the newfound skills among a group of fellow artisans, and ultimately, internalize the capabilities as intangible personal resources for change beyond the workshops. Figure 8.1 depicts the evolving process from concrete capabilities on the left as they transform to increasingly abstract, intangible capabilities on the right. Moving across, artisans evolve from passive receivers of skills to active agents of change in the group, household, and community.

Upon joining a MarketPlace workshop, artisans acquire new skills that enlarge both their economic and social capabilities. As artisans learn technical skills to cut, sew, and embroider MarketPlace garments, they also gain experience in recording operations, maintaining records and inspecting garments for quality features. Information shared with the artisans about consumer preferences from customers halfway around the globe challenged the artisans' thinking about their long-internalized Indian aesthetics. Not only do artisans work within the workshop or home setting, but they also travel beyond their neighborhood lanes to deliver and collect materials from the MarketPlace office at the edge of the slum. Learning these technical skills is accompanied by opportunities to broaden social and interpersonal capabilities as well. Reading, writing, using the telephone, and expressing opinions offer paths for expanded ability to interact with others. Learning to use public transportation (such as buses and trains) affords opportunities to go outside the slums to procure supplies (buttons, zippers, threads, etc.) and across the city to visit other workshops.

At a next level of abstraction, concrete economic and social capabilities extend as women work together in applying their newly acquired expertise. Artisans begin to understand that their individual actions affect outcomes for the entire workshop. Women engage in more complex processes of production planning, including adoption of value-added activities. Artisans become managers as they rearrange their workshops for greater production efficiencies and learn to solve the inevitable problems that arise when assembling garments. Women no longer are merely provided work to complete. Rather, they actively employ their newly acquired interpersonal communication skills and their enhanced capacity to work jointly in achieving the workshop's goals of delivering orders on time.

As women achieve success in producing and delivering MarketPlace garments, capabilities are internalized as intangible resources for broader engagement as agents of change within the home and neighborhood. What began as concrete income-generating and communication skills evolve into more abstract qualities of self-respect, confidence, and courage. Artisans' life perspectives evolve from mother and wife to that of income providers and persons with immense potential to impact the lives of others around them. As capabilities expand, the artisan's worldview enlarges from the household to the broader neighborhood and city of Mumbai.

Our assessment of MarketPlace artisan capabilities offers both comparisons and contrasts with other scholars who have focused on capability acquisition and enactment, and on human agency. Clearly, MarketPlace's approach to fair trade couples the acquisition *and* application of capabilities as advocated by Sen (1980). Ongoing skill development is central to MarketPlace work. However, the workshop members must also creatively combine their capabilities and, over time and by trial and error, develop a process whereby their groups of artisans can work together to plan, produce, and deliver garments. The evolving systems differ from group to group; no format mirrors that of another group. For those workshop leaders who have gone on to form new offshoot businesses, the application of capabilities expands even further.

The capabilities acquired and applied at MarketPlace compare closely with five of the nine capabilities espoused by Nussbaum (2000) as central, interconnected components of human functioning. As women carry out work in MarketPlace workshops, they "imagine, sense, and reason," acquire emotional attachments to other people "without overwhelming fear or anxiety," "engage in critical reflection about the planning of one's life," participate in social interactions where they show concern for others and are "treated as dignified beings with worth equal to others," and experience some control over their lives by "having the right to seek employment on an equal basis with others" (78-80).

While the acquisition and application of capabilities at MarketPlace support the work of Nussbaum and Sen (1993), they offer an opportunity to expand on Hill's (2001) assertion that agency precedes capability acquisition. Hill defines *agency* as the ability to act that is predicated on self- and interpersonal respect acquired through solidarity and collective action. Our findings from MarketPlace suggest a different picture that emerges by separating capability acquisition into both concrete and intangible formats and by inserting group action in setting and meeting goals (see Figure 8.1). Capability acquisition and agency evolve hand in hand rather than capability acquisition emerging as an outgrowth of agency. At MarketPlace, concrete capabilities are first individually acquired and then collectively applied in a group setting (agency) to the planning and execution of the group's apparel production goals, a process that assists in the transformation of concrete skills to more abstract capabilities of planning and management. These intangible capabilities are internalized into resources for further action (agency), this time in support of the group, household, and beyond.

We contend that the fair trade model, as practiced by MarketPlace, with its concern for both the economic and social development of artisans is central to this process. Within the fair trade model, dual concern for capability acquisition and broader social development occur simultaneously. Fair trade organizations attend not only to the wages of workers and what a group produces but also how the production is carried out in support of holistic development of the artisans. Under the fair trade premise, the longer-term perspective in working with artisans contributes to opportunity for the evolution of capability acquisition, application, and transformation as evidenced by MarketPlace.

Livelihood

Economic livelihood requires dependable sources of cash and food that cover basic needs for existence and is essential to well-being (Chambers 1997). MarketPlace provides artisans, limited in capabilities and options, the opportunity to earn an income by sewing and embroidering apparel that has appeal to a market segment of US consumers. Admirably, MarketPlace, as a fair trade organization, seeks not simply to employ a stable workforce for reliable production of its apparel but instead focuses on putting income into the hands of some of India's most poor and vulnerable individuals. The income earned by these artisans makes critical contributions to covering a share of the artisans' households' most basic expenses for housing, food, utilities, and others. In some cases, artisans are able to save a bit of money or have enough earnings that they can use discretion in buying products that enhance their lives and reduce the burden of everyday responsibilities. While expanding and applying their capabilities, the women working with MarketPlace are able to address some of their most basic physiological needs for food and housing. The artisans for the most part believe they are paid fairly, and they perceive their lives are much better as a result of their work. We agree that without a doubt, MarketPlace artisans and their families are better off because of their employment with the fair trade organization.

Chambers notes that an essential characteristic of economic livelihood is that it be "dependable." Yet, seasonal fluctuations plague the fair trade organization. MarketPlace artisans face spikes and dips in production and corresponding peaks and valleys in pay that diminish the dependability of their earnings. The dependability of the artisans' incomes is further diminished when the available work is spread out thinly across many artisan members. How to increase the dependability of earnings and decrease the level of underemployment among those artisans wishing to work more is worthy of examination.

The "difficulties of tailoring supply to (highly fluctuating) demand" is a systemic issue occurring for over 100 years in the mainstream apparel industry (Green 2003, 37). The way major apparel brands and retailers have dealt with seasonality is to outsource assembly of garments to factories that are then contracted for production on a transactional basis. Long and multitiered supply chains comprising contractors, subcontractors, home-workers, and others have resulted: the problem of seasonality as an industry responsibility to the labor force is passed down the supply chain (Green 2003; Hurley 2005). The situation is exacerbated by contractor specialization (different equipment is required to make lightweight cotton dresses and jackets, for example, as compared with down parkas), changes in weather, economic downturns and recessions, and consumer preferences. The outcomes to workers in the mainstream apparel industry have been grim; they often experience job insecurity, short-term contracts, little power or control in the work relationship, and low wages that are incompletely paid or paid late (Hurley 2005).

The situation of seasonality, underemployment, and homework observed with MarketPlace and the artisans we studied is very different from that of the mainstream apparel industry. The supply chain is much shorter, the power relationships are intentionally as balanced as possible, and the orders are more consistent over the long term. The homework we observed does not stem from denial of responsibility by employers, but rather the realities of space and life in the slums of Mumbai, and as Green (2003) has noted,

> importantly provides work for some people who would otherwise be excluded from the labor market. Women with children, an unemployed husband, sick parents, or cultural traditions that make it difficult to work outside the home, have often turned to homework to contribute to the family budget. (47)

While MarketPlace has attempted to lessen the impacts of seasonal demand by spreading out orders for goods across a several month period as described in Chapter 3, and assisting the groups to identify and develop local markets for production that could be completed when MarketPlace orders are low, challenges remain. Particularly, Pushpika notes that the organization's commitment to using handprinted fabric can result in delays in obtaining raw materials and bottlenecks in production. Monsoons and humid weather conditions, for example, do not allow the fabric to dry quickly after printing. Purchases of only small quantities of dyes at a time, due to dye costs and uncertainty in demand, increase the likelihood of colors failing to meet standards in subsequent orders. Artisans based in rural areas often balance the seasonal nature of demand from tourist and other markets with agricultural work (Milgram 2000); this strategy is clearly not an option to artisans residing in urban slum areas.

Given the common negative impacts that seasonal production has on workers who sew garments for major brands and retailers, and artisans who sew and embroider apparel and household products for the fair trade organization, we believe this intersection provides an important area for future collaboration and investigation. Workers and artisans have much to gain from mainstream brands and retailers, fair trade organizations, consumer behavior researchers, social scientists and anthropologists, business management specialists, industrial engineers, development agencies, and others working together to find a solution to seasonal variation in demand and the negative impacts it has on wages and job security. Fair trade organizations, with their history of offering alternative solutions to problems found in global trade, could logically take leadership in an initiative to change the model for how businesses respond to consumer demand. Similarly, joint efforts could be made to define and recognize homework that is appropriate and necessary from that which is not.

While economic livelihood has not been and should not be the sole focus of MarketPlace, it should, perhaps, be given greater consideration in the future. While MarketPlace has been careful to balance the products it develops to incorporate both embroidery and sewing in the interest of employing a range of artisans and to create uncomplicated embroidery designs that are simple for the women to complete, there would be benefits from also working to upgrade the skills of embroiderers to take on the more advanced work of sewing apparel. In addition, because MarketPlace has made it a high priority to provide some income for very poor artisans with minimal skills, the skill levels of those embroidering its products are highly varied. It is likely that at least some artisans are unable to earn the hourly wages MarketPlace sets on the basis of average skill levels. Apparel factories likely avoid this problem simply by employing only those with higher and more similar skills and not hiring or firing those who cannot reach a minimum level of productivity—this is clearly not a compatible option for the MarketPlace groups who select artisan members primarily on the basis of need. Perhaps the groups could experiment with different work roles and responsibilities that might better suit those unable to meet certain minimum levels of productivity. Some women might be much more qualified and productive (and able to earn minimum wages expected by MarketPlace) in quality control, packing and shipping, and sourcing roles.

Well-Being

Chambers asserts that well-being should be viewed from four perspectives. While we explored indicators for material, psychological, and social well-being, we did not attempt to address spiritual indicators. MarketPlace's holistic perspective on women's lives, inside the workshop and beyond, clearly acknowledges that women are physical, emotional, and social beings. As shown in Figure 8.2, artisan's well-being encompasses a broad range of life changes. Interestingly, when we first met with the MarketPlace women to discuss our interest in "telling the MarketPlace story," the topics that the women identified for inclusion in our interviews encompassed Chambers's multiple perspectives for defining well-being.

As depicted in Figure 8.2, we do not conceptualize the forms of well-being as evolving sequentially, but rather each interacts with and sustains the others. For example, as women find a supportive environment in which they can think toward and even dream about a future (psychological), their hopes for and confidence in making decisions about their children's education

Figure 8.2 Material, psychological, and social indicators of MarketPlace artisan well-being.

Material
*Housing
*Diet, health care
*Education
*Consumer products
*Clothng
*Bank accounts

Artisan Well-being

Social
*Friendship with other women
*Decision making for children
*Community respect

Psychological
*Freedom from fear, worry, loneliness, and isolation
* Relaxation from household tensions
*Ability to dream

Global Dialogue

Identity, strong women, transitions, differences, community, beauty

Community Action

Sanitation, food rations, and health care

surface (social). Interest in enhanced personal appearance (material) follows as women gain community respect and show pride in new friendships (social), and rid themselves of loneliness (psychological).

The MarketPlace approach for well-being clearly illustrates the Indian model of high-impact, all-female NGOs proposed by Handy, Kassam,

Feeney, and Ranade in 2006. The capabilities acquired at MarketPlace, and the enhanced ability to provide for family livelihood, contribute toward a woman who not only participates in and helps to manage a small business but also "can eventually effectively navigate [her] way in the sociocultural environment in which she functions" (130). MarketPlace founders, as with other organizations that have accomplished this goal, hold fast to promotion of social justice, particularly as related to women and their empowerment. They have established collaborative and inclusive workplaces where artisans are involved in decision making and learn to experience the impacts that their decisions can have on others. Pushpika Freitas and Lalita Monteiro, MarketPlace founders and sisters, honed and internalized a perspective on social justice within their own supportive family where they experienced, on a daily basis, the importance of helping others through social work programs. Promoting social justice was not an academic concept learned in school but nurtured on a daily basis through role models at home. The young women's higher education training in social work (Pushpika) and business accounting (Lalita) provided further grounding upon which they could draw as MarketPlace grew and evolved.

In addition to strong female leaders, MarketPlace also illustrates high vertical integration in its programs and services intended to promote holistic development within the organization (Handy et al. 2006). While MarketPlace incorporated economic and social programs from the outset, frequent additions or modification of programs complemented the core activities as the organization evolved. For example, an early educational sponsorship program from US customers for artisans' children was replaced with the Armaan Club. As the artisan's urgent financial need for their children's schooling lessened and the children became older, they expressed interest in after school enrichment activities. The multiplier effects of these sequential activities included several of the high school age children serving as assistants for our research interviews. Others have pursued postsecondary training in computers or gone on to college. In a second example, recent recreational field trips and "activity days" go beyond the comfort and support established by members within their workshops by providing a chance to physically get away from the slums, play, laugh, and relax for a day.

MarketPlace also illustrates an organization with generational programs (Handy et al. 2006; Korten 1987). Generational activities come about as an organization and its members broaden their worldview of how they can impact others beyond the group through advocacy, enhanced capacity, and decision making. As noted in Figure 8.2, both the global dialogue and community action programs, initiated early in MarketPlace's history as part of their vertical integration, have expanded as the women's frames of reference have enlarged. For example, the women who gather for Global Dialogue discussions now approach complex topics such as the practice of dowry, the meaning of human beauty, or living in harmony with nature, all of which illustrate an awareness of their potential for impact in a world beyond the slum. In a second example, responding to a specific request from the artisans for information on their legal rights as women, MarketPlace partnered with a sister NGO for the artisans to attend weekly discussions on women and the law. Initial sessions were one-sided with the trainers providing information to the artisans. However, by the time the program ended, the artisans eagerly participated with a range of specific questions and perspectives that reflected their expanded vision of what their lives could be.

As we stated in Chapter 2, quality of life is complex and multi-dimensional. Insights gained from assessing artisans' capabilities, livelihood, and well-being certainly confirm this initial assessment. Had we used only one or two indicators, a partial picture would have emerged. Examining capabilities or well-being present a more positive outlook for quality of life than looking solely at livelihood. As noted in previous research (Biswas-Diener and Diener 2001), the MarketPlace women appear to be using their strong social skills and intergroup support to "counterbalance" some of the "negative effects of poverty." These women's personal confidence and social networks would not be in place without the training and support received from their work at MarketPlace. Improved quality of life as voiced by the MarketPlace women strongly supports the fair trade enterprise's dual-focused approach on income generation and social development. Having the opportunity to work at MarketPlace initiates artisans' journeys toward an improved quality of life. While the artisans continue to voice economic concerns, these challenges seem balanced by strides made in other aspects of life.

Fair Trade Apparel Certification and MarketPlace

A third set of research questions asked what artisans working with MarketPlace stand to gain or lose from fair trade apparel or organizational certification and as a result, what recommendations could we make to these organizations based on the MarketPlace experience? Our discussion focuses first on assessing whether MarketPlace or its groups might be able to obtain fair trade certification for its apparel products or its organizational practices. We then consider the advantages and disadvantages of certification. We end this section by developing recommendations for the fair trade labeling organizations that are experimenting with fair trade apparel product certification (such as Transfair USA) in hopes that our guidance will allow them to develop policies that support and improve the fair trade policies and practices of MarketPlace and other small apparel producers. In the final section, we likewise develop recommendations for organizations developing standards for fair trade organizational certification, particularly the WFTO (World Fair Trade Organization).

Could MarketPlace and Its Artisan Groups Earn Fair Trade Apparel or Organizational Certification?

Two proposed programs, Transfair USA's draft fair trade apparel certification program and the WFTO's Sustainable Fair Trade Management System (SFTMS), provide possibilities such that in the near future both Market-Place and its artisan groups could seek certification of its fair trade *products* or *business practices*. Under the emerging Transfair USA model for *product* certification, it appears that MarketPlace itself would have the option of seeking certification as a buyer of fair trade apparel and household textiles, but we question whether the guidelines are appropriately set for small organizations. It is clear that MarketPlace would have no trouble demonstrating that it maintains long-term and stable relationships with the groups. However, MarketPlace would need to make sure its groups are using fair trade certified cotton in all their products. It is uncertain whether MarketPlace groups would be able to purchase fair trade cotton, as it is produced in limited supplies and would require careful tracing of the commodity as it is ginned and woven into base goods. The artisan groups and fabric suppliers would need to undergo inspection and comply with the Transfair USA standards. MarketPlace would also need to pay a fair trade premium to all the groups involved, including the cotton producers. At least for the artisan groups that we studied, it may be possible to link the development work that is carried out within the groups to this premium, as long as workers decide what to fund with the premium.

In addition to MarketPlace itself, the artisan groups with which it works would have the option of pursuing Transfair USA *product* certification. However, the labeling organization's focus on larger, more industrial cut-make-trim (CMT) facilities means that many of the standards set are incompatible with the physical and human resource realities surrounding the very small workshops operating under the MarketPlace umbrella.

For example, although we are not specialists in environmental health and safety, by nature of their location in Mumbai's slums, the workshops contain health and safety risks that are easily observed. Workshops tend to be cramped, haphazardly wired for electricity, are sometimes poorly lit, and have no toilet facilities available in the workshop; nearby slum latrines are unhygienic. None of these conditions would be compliant with Transfair

USA's (2009) standards. Furthermore, homeworking arrangements, which are prevalent and necessary within the MarketPlace workshops, are not allowed under Transfair USA's draft proposal. Some of the groups are not cooperatively organized, although all groups involve extensive artisan participation in decision making and would surely score high on Transfair USA's standards for worker participation.

The lack of records on hours worked by each artisan would make it difficult for the groups to demonstrate compliance with the maximum hours of work stipulated by Transfair USA. Similarly, while there would likely be no issues with forced labor or child labor, the MarketPlace workshops may not maintain adequate documentation to satisfy monitors that workers meet minimum age requirements under Transfair USA standards. In fact, when interviewing the women for this study, we had to ask for approximate ages, as many of the women did not know their ages. On the plus side, given their great respect to individuals and the most vulnerable in society, the workshops would likely score well on nondiscrimination, disciplinary practices, and women's rights. However, we question how a twenty-person workshop in a slum in India, or in the Highlands of Guatemala for that matter, can be evaluated on the same criteria as an industrial factory with 500 workers.

In contrast to Transfair's product certification program, MarketPlace and its workshops have a much greater likelihood of earning *organizational certification* under the WFTO's SFTMS standards. These standards have been developed with small organizations in mind. MarketPlace creates opportunities for economically disadvantaged artisans, providing them with greater independence and expanded capabilities for work. Extensive information is provided to consumers about the organization's products and producers, and quality control is emphasized in the production of those goods. MarketPlace champions women, respecting and valuing their work at all levels. The organization builds long-term relationships with its workshops, operating with trust and solidarity to the artisans' benefit. Marketplace pays fair wages in the local context.

Gains and Losses to Marketplace From Certification

What is to be potentially gained and lost by the artisans of MarketPlace or its groups should they be able or unable to achieve fair trade apparel or organizational certification? Certification programs have considerable value under increasing calls for accountability by consumers and societal groups. Thus, if MarketPlace and its groups could obtain certification from one or both programs, they would gain greater credibility in the eyes of the public. As more products and organizations are certified as being produced under fair trade principles, the absence of certification will become noticeable to the growing base of consumers who use certification as a tool for gathering prepurchase information.

Attempting to achieve certification in a product-oriented program that is not appropriately aligned with the needs of small producers and with the development focus of the organization, however, would probably be costly to MarketPlace and its groups. Trying to achieve certification under Transfair USA's 2009 draft apparel standard would likely require that MarketPlace shift resources from development activities that have contributed to the essence of MarketPlace and immense social growth in the artisans to premium payments. It is unclear whether MarketPlace and its groups could continue to assist additional vulnerable individuals in obtaining much-needed work in the future. Their artisans' limited interpersonal experiences and capabilities for work necessitate the type of development work that MarketPlace and its social work organization, SHARE, have championed. In addition, without creation of more relevant standards aligned with the local context, homework that meshes well with the artisans' family responsibilities would need to end—artisans would likely need to report to work at a central location where workplace conditions and hours could be more closely controlled and monitored. It is unclear to us how the women we interviewed could accommodate this type of schedule given the current context of their lives where work and household responsibilities must be interspersed. Furthermore, there would seem to be no physical space in close proximity to the artisans' homes to house such a factory. We fear that important development practices that have led to remarkable advances in the lives of the MarketPlace artisans would lose relevance under a program that did not appropriately recognize the life context and advances in development of fair trade groups that have been operating for decades.

Obtaining WFTO certification at the organizational level would be a better fit and would provide advantages to MarketPlace. The organization would be able to credibly claim 100% Fair Trade status and differentiate itself from businesses practicing "fair trade lite." SFTMS certification would provide a publicly visible way to verify compliance to a clear set of goals, and position MarketPlace to address what Conroy (2007) describes as the growing public interest in accountability.

Recommendations for Fair Trade Apparel Certification

We believe that at this point, the MarketPlace organization and its workshops would find it nearly impossible to earn certification that its *apparel products* are made under fair trade practices because an applicable set of standards for small organizations such as MarketPlace has not been created. The Transfair USA (2009) draft standard for Fair Trade Certified Apparel and Home Goods includes rigorous standards based on conventions of the International Labour Organization (ILO) and is aimed primarily toward large-scale CMT factories with industrial settings. Would preventing organizations such as MarketPlace that work with small producers from earning certification assist the fair trade movement? We think not. We strongly encourage Transfair USA to move quickly to establish a second set of standards and benchmarks for certifying fair trade apparel that is produced in small workshops and even in homework settings. The current draft standards and benchmarks are simply too far removed from the contextual realities of smaller artisan groups such as those we have described in this book and that are prevalent in fair trade. Standards for small producers do not need to be as rigorous as those for large-scale, industrial producers. Rather, the standards for small producers need to be the right standards, reflecting the workers' current economic and social situations and what would move them toward greater empowerment, expanded earnings, and taking more meaningful roles in their families and communities.

We also encourage certifying bodies to incorporate standards for measuring noneconomic, social benefits for producers, which will more closely align fair trade product certification standards with what has been the heart and soul of the fair trade movement since its initiation in the 1950s. By embracing a fair trade development mission, organizations are capable of making significant social and economic impacts on the most vulnerable individuals. One way to do this might involve creating metrics to identify the social benefits gained from the fair trade premium. As we did with the research we present in this book, the workers themselves could be asked to determine appropriate standards. Expanding accountability for social development would prevent ongoing criticism that fair trade has been reduced to a single issue of fair price or "fair trade lite" (see Gogoi 2008). Measuring development benefits does not meet the call made by Robinson and Athreya (2005) to develop "a simple criterion" to certify producers and easily connect them "with conscientious consumers" (8). However, MarketPlace has demonstrated through the strong links it fosters between consumers and artisans in its Global Dialogue program that consumers are capable of understanding the value and impact of development activities. Especially when considering small producers, assessment of development activities would serve as a point of differentiation between them and large producers who are working with people with a greater range of life experiences, more capabilities, and varied development needs.

Finally, we urge Transfair USA and other labeling organizations to consider other possible criteria for determining whether freedom of association and collective-bargaining rights are upheld. Mukherjee and Reed (2009) have raised concerns about focusing on increasing fair trade workers' ability to use industrial relations mechanisms and negotiate pay and working conditions, rather than involving them in decisions related more to the business of fair trade. As we considered the variety of activities that MarketPlace workshops were engaged in, we were mindful that despite the remarkable ways women were being empowered, some MarketPlace groups do not meet the emerging fair trade apparel certification program's requirements for demonstrating empowerment.

As indicated in Chapter 3, a group leader in one of the cooperatively organized artisan groups had stolen money and equipment from the group before it joined MarketPlace. We have observed similar corruption within cooperatives in other countries as well. It seems possible that there are varied strategies for ensuring that workers are provided appropriate voice in the policies and practices that impact them. Workers should certainly not be prevented from forming unions should that be their preference, and at this stage in their development it would seem important for MarketPlace and other fair trade organizations to expose workers to their rights as individuals and also as workers. However, in a fair trade organization that focuses on assisting the desperately poor, not all workers will have the confidence and capabilities necessary to take leadership roles in their organizations. We believe that the capabilities and agency being developed among women working with MarketPlace are fundamental to their longer-term attainment of human and worker rights.

Knowledge Gained From the Global Apparel Industry's Efforts to Address Worker and Human Rights

Our fourth set of questions concerns what 100% Fair Trade organizations such as MarketPlace can learn from the global apparel industry's decade-long effort to address worker and human rights. The bar has been set high by apparel industry stakeholders with businesses needing to ensure workers are provided the rights outlined in ILO conventions in order to be considered socially responsible. In this section, we address this question and provide fair trade organizations (such as the WFTO) with recommendations for new policies and practices to adopt in their fair trade missions.

What Fair Trade Organizations Can Learn From the Global Apparel Industry

Apparel brands and retailers first realized in the late 1980s and early 1990s that they had a growing problem with labor standards and working conditions in factories making their products around the world. After a period where companies denied responsibility, many brands and retailers began developing codes of conduct for labor standards and working conditions with which their contracted factories would be expected to comply. Early codes of conduct were somewhat vague, but as social responsibility expanded, the codes were increasingly aligned with internationally agreed-upon labor standards and the rights of workers were connected with human rights every individual is afforded (Dickson, Loker, and Eckman 2009). The connection of apparel industry codes of conduct to human and worker rights has been invaluable for clarifying appropriate standards that all businesses should work to provide those who labor for their benefit. Likewise, the 100% Fair Trade movement would benefit from identifying clear and measurable standards for the workplace that serve to move workers in these small enterprises closer to the basic rights and freedoms they deserve. Organizations like MarketPlace and the larger umbrella WFTO should seek to explicitly connect their standards with universally agreed human and worker rights. This does not mean they should adopt the exact standards and benchmarks of larger multinational corporations and industrial workplaces. Rather, fair trade organizations with a development focus will need to customize their standards to appropriately link with the development levels in the regions and countries in which they operate and prioritize the problems they tackle first (Office of the United Nations High Commissioner for Human Rights 2006). Then, much as the multinational apparel brands of the 1990s realized was necessary, fair trade organizations must recognize that to make progress toward those goals will require adopting methods to measure progress, to continually redefine strategies for improvement toward the goals, and transparently report the progress they are making toward their goals and the difficulties they are encountering (see Dickson, Loker, and Eckman 2009). Small organizations will likely require capacity building for developing the human resource management systems necessary to track progress.

Recommendations for Fair Trade Organizational Certifying Bodies

The WFTO organizational certification for 100% Fair Trade businesses holds promise for MarketPlace and similar small producer groups. However, as the processes for verifying compliance to the standards are just being developed, now is an excellent time to ensure that the certification program will support artisan groups as they strive to improve their lives by accessing lucrative markets around the world. We center our focus on three key areas—tackling the problem of underemployment, determining metrics for assessing worker empowerment, and public accountability.

Fair trade as it was originally envisioned by organizations such as Ten Thousand Villages and SERRV placed high priority on development activities. Fair trade leaders, including Pushpika with MarketPlace, have worked hard to prevent the artisan groups with which they work from becoming dependent on their single organizations for all of the groups' orders. Groups are expected to pursue other buyers and other markets to develop a steady flow of work to keep artisans fully employed; yet, sometimes groups lack the entrepreneurial skills or will to do this. We believe the WFTO and its member fair trade organizations should collaboratively work to tackle this issue. The systemic problem is beyond what one fair trade organization can solve, but in collaboration with other fair trade organizations, governments, academics, and others, there would certainly be possible solutions that could be explored.

Similarly, fair trade organizations and the WFTO should also carry out collaborative discussions with stakeholders about mutually agreeable measures for worker empowerment. The activism we observed among women working with MarketPlace demonstrated an amazing level of empowerment, although it was focused on community rather than labor rights. Perhaps labor rights education could be incorporated into some of the development activities pursued by fair trade organizations.

At the beginning of this century, when MarketPlace asked us to audit the impacts their work had on the artisans, they ushered in a new era of accountability among fair trade organizations and for that matter the apparel industry. The organization's willingness to let us delve into their work practices and share publicly the outcomes is progressive. This level of public accountability should be applauded as a leadership activity defining social responsibility. This level of transparency represents what Ed Williams, head of Corporate Social Responsibility for the British retail leader Marks and Spencer, claims is a growing trend that businesses must prove to their stakeholders that they carry out the socially responsible actions they tout (Conroy 2007). We look forward to other fair trade organizations, as well as mainstream apparel brands and retailers, expanding their accountability and transparency in the future.

Fair Trade Artisan Work: Survival or Asset Building?

In the final set of questions, we turn to the queries and concerns raised by researchers, development experts, and artisan leaders who have asked if and how artisan work contributes to artisans' lives. They question whether artisan work is a survival or asset-building strategy. Along with heads of NGOs and trade unions, they share concerns that all work be "decent work." We end our book by addressing these concerns.

In assessing whether artisan work is a survival or asset-building strategy, our answer, from close inspection of MarketPlace artisans' lives, is that it is not an either/or situation. Instead, fair trade artisan work as practiced at Marketplace is both. Despite the income brought home from MarketPlace, underemployment is evident and most households still struggle to meet their monthly expenses. Yet the women, most of whom did not have jobs before joining MarketPlace, assess that they are providing for their families significantly better than before joining the organization. The artisans articulate a broad range of assets they have gained at MarketPlace. Assets range from skills and confidence for making household decisions, particularly those that will turn their children's lives toward new directions, to conviction for speaking up and taking action on behalf of other women and for their communities.

MarketPlace embodies the core mission of fair trade in working with disadvantaged individuals in small enterprises and over a sustained period of time. A small enterprise encourages leadership to develop broadly among its members and not just among a few supervisors. Through sustained commitment, artisans have time to acquire and then to hone new capabilities for wide-ranging application. These core characteristics of small size and prolonged commitment seem essential for fair trade to reach goals of capacity building. Small workshops and opportunities to work from the home retain a fit with the context of women's lives in settings such as the slums of Mumbai. These small workshops provide opportunities for women who would be unable to work in large industrial factories.

We end the book by assessing whether MarketPlace and its small artisan groups provide "decent work." Decent work is not defined by the size of the workshop or factory, but rather the practices within the business or organization and the relationships between individuals. Decent work allows all people to attain internationally recognized human rights (ILO 2007). It provides people with hope and aspirations that encompass opportunities for income, "rights, voice and recognition; family stability and personal development; and fairness and gender equality" (ILO, n.d). We strongly believe that MarketPlace indeed provides decent work. The organization is "helping individuals obtain life skills that will assist them in obtaining work, preventing discrimination, and increasing women's participation in work." It is

> providing skills training, meeting the demands of the labor market, involving workers . . . in designing training programs, creating opportunities to increase income earning capacity of specific disadvantaged or marginalized groups, including informal workers, people in rural areas, poor women, people with disabilities, and others. (ILO 2007)

Furthermore, MarketPlace is "helping people be citizens, and enhance their culture, education, family, and community," which results in a more holistic improvement of the workers' lives across the lifecycle (ILO 2007). The women we met, who sew and embroider MarketPlace goods, shared their deepest challenges and their most cherished goals. MarketPlace: Handwork of India artisans are clearly engaged in decent work.

Appendix: Methods

I n our earlier book, *Social Responsibility in the Global Market: Fair Trade of Cultural Products,* we proposed that "fair trade fosters empowerment and improved quality of life for artisan producers through an integrated and sustained system of trade partnerships among producers, retailers, and consumers" (Littrell and Dickson 1999, 5). While we and others involved in the fair trade movement can cite substantial anecdotal evidence to support this statement, comprehensive empirical assessment was missing. *Artisans and Fair Trade* offers the first in-depth critique of social and economic impacts of fair trade artisan work. This appendix documents the case study methodology we employed for assessing fair trade accountability. As is common in case study research, we drew upon multiple sources of data from interviews, field observations, and photodocumentation to tap the multifaceted experiences of artisans working for MarketPlace: Handwork of India (MarketPlace).

Early Contacts With MarketPlace

Our multiyear journey with MarketPlace began in 1992 when we first met Pushpika Freitas at a Fair Trade Conference in Vermont. We found Pushpika's story to be engaging for its coupling of women artisans' economic and social development from the organization's outset, the urban setting in Mumbai, India, and the unique MarketPlace apparel items, with their hallmark of handcrafted fabrics embellished with surface embroidery. In contrast, other fair trade organizations with which we were familiar frequently added social or community dimensions after business start-up, worked with artisans in rural areas, and shied away from clothing production due to fit and sizing issues.

In the ensuing years, we engaged with Pushpika, her sisters Lalita and Indira, and the SHARE (Support the Handicapped's Rehabilitation Effort) social workers Fatima Merchant and Devi Nair, in meeting the MarketPlace artisans, deepening our understanding of the MarketPlace business and design processes, and learning about MarketPlace customers.

Prior to the research upon which this book is based, Mary made two trips to MarketPlace in Mumbai. In 1996, Mary conducted participant observation research during an intense two-week design and product review for a forthcoming MarketPlace catalog. Participation in the design workshop held in Bhavnigar afforded many opportunities to experience the concentrated activities of fabric selection, garment design, and embroidery innovation that surround the evolution of a MarketPlace apparel line. Back in Mumbai, Mary visited each of the MarketPlace producer groups where she interviewed artisans and observed their production. On a near-daily basis, she was invited to return home with artisans to meet their families, discuss daily routines, and observe first-hand the conditions in which women embroider MarketPlace products. Again, in 2000, Mary returned to India to meet with each of the artisan groups to introduce the upcoming Earthwatch project for this book and to ascertain their willingness to participate in interviews. Overwhelmingly, the artisans voiced their readiness to "tell their story" about life and work at MarketPlace, at home, and in their neighborhoods.

In addition to becoming familiar with the Marketplace leaders and artisans, we gained insights into MarketPlace customer demand. Market research was conducted with the organization's customers on three occasions. First, in 1996, two doctoral students from Iowa State University, Jennifer Ogle and Soyoung Kim, provided assistance in questionnaire design, data collection, and analysis. A total of 477 individuals, drawn from the Market-Place nationwide mailing list, provided insights concerning the customer's values, attitudes toward fair trade, and their clothing and shopping preferences. In a second survey in 2003-2004, MarketPlace joined with three other prominent fair trade organizations (Equal Exchange, SERRV, and Ten Thousand Villages) for a North American survey (United States and Canada) for investigating whether there was a common core of values and behaviors among their fair trade customers. Iowa State University doctoral students Jaya Halepete and Yoon Jin Ma served as research assistants for this second project. Finally, in 2005, Jaya Halepete conducted her dissertation research with MarketPlace customers, focusing on their interest in acquiring apparel that was personalized to their aesthetic taste and body size.

Across these surveys, we ascertained the importance that MarketPlace's customers placed on paying fair wages and on treatment of artisans. The MarketPlace story engaged their interest and allowed them to act on their values. However, while customers valued the organization's mission, they were also insistent that the apparel be of high quality and meet their aesthetic criteria in order for them to make repeat purchases. Together, immersion in the MarketPlace supply chain from interviews with fabric producers and apparel artisans to surveys of final customers provided a holistic picture of the multiple issues facing a fair trade organization and provided a rich context for the in-depth interviews to be conducted for this book.

Earthwatch Institute Funding

The Earthwatch Institute based in Maynard, Massachusetts, provided funding for our research. Earthwatch is one of the world's leading environmental research organizations. Along with studies on ecosystems, climate change, and oceans, research that addresses the world's cultural heritage (e.g., artisan work in India) is included in their priority areas for funding. As a criterion for Earthwatch Institute funding, volunteer research assistants must be intimately involved in collection of field data. Earthwatch describes their research approach.

> We use a unique model of citizen science, matching volunteers with researchers to investigate some of the greatest environmental challenges facing our planet. Earthwatch is dedicated to creating an environmental legacy through scientific research projects, education, and learning opportunities, and engaging people in field research (Earthwatch Fact Sheet 2009).

Across the two years of our field research, three teams of volunteers joined us in Mumbai for periods of two weeks. The twenty-four volunteers (twenty-one women and three men) arrived from four countries (Australia, Canada, England, and the United States) and ranged in age from eighteen to eighty-two years. Volunteers' life experiences ranged from a student who had recently completing a bachelor's degree at Harvard University to a retired psychotherapist, a dietician, a few teachers, and a volunteer who had just sold his dot.com business for a sizeable profit and was searching for ways to launch a social capital venture.

Prior to beginning their interviews, volunteers received two and one-half days of training with the researchers to familiarize them with MarketPlace and SHARE. Training and discussion centered on four major topic areas:

1) Overview of MarketPlace, SHARE, the MarketPlace product development process, and fair trade

2) Insights into women's lives in Mumbai, an overview of specific artisan groups, and the Golibar slum, including home visits with some of the artisans they would be interviewing

3) Research skills for interviewing, note taking, photodocumentation, and computer data entry

4) Culturally appropriate behaviors for interacting with Indian women; for example, shoes are always removed when entering a MarketPlace workshop or artisan's home

In addition to our instruction, training was conducted by Fatima Merchant, Executive Director of SHARE, and Devi Nair, the Associate Director. In order to broaden volunteers' perspectives on other development projects, on two evenings we visited several NGOs that work with street children, homosexuals, and women's issues. On Saturday, midway through each team visit, lecturers introduced various Indian religions, followed by a city tour of Mumbai.

Interviews

The interview protocol for collecting artisans' life stories and for exploring their experiences with MarketPlace was developed collaboratively among the MarketPlace leaders, the artisans, and ourselves. Artisans, many of whom had been with MarketPlace for a number of years, suggested a variety of social indicators they believed should be included for telling their personal and MarketPlace stories. This strategy followed recommendations from scholars involved in development work that variables related to Basic Human Needs and well-being must be "defined by the locals" (Brinkerhoff, Fredell, and Frideres 1997, 252). Salient capabilities and dimensions of well-being identified by the artisans included influence on decision making in the household, social status in their neighborhoods, self-confidence and self-improvement, economic independence, and awareness of social issues. From the outset, the artisans alerted us to the importance of using multiple indicators for assessing the impacts of MarketPlace work on their lives. The artisan-suggested topics were coupled with questions we drew from our previous research and from scholarship associated with the research questions introduced in Chapter 1. In particular, research on global development, artisan traditions, apparel product development, household economics in international settings, and quality of life formed a foundation from which questions were developed.

In order that we could apply the development model introduced by Robert Chambers (see Chapter 2), it was important that we include questions to assess economic livelihood and material well-being as identified in his model. Measures of economic livelihood included open- and close-ended items about artisan monthly wages, household income provided by spouse and other household members, whether artisans had saved money, and average monthly expenditures for a variety of essential household products and services. When inquiring about income for all householders, we asked artisans to indicate both the maximum and the minimum income each person contributed per month. This measure of income recognizes that many jobs do not provide a steady income, rather the income varies with production cycles or other seasonal fluctuations.

Material well-being was measured in multiple ways. Artisans reported monthly expenses for housing, food, transportation, utilities (cooking fuel, water, and electricity), and entertainment. In addition, annual expenses were reported for medical needs, education, clothing, and travel home. An objective Basic Minimum Needs ratio was generated by dividing total household income by average monthly expenditures on food, housing, transportation, and utilities. The Basic Minimum Needs ratio identified the extent that basic needs were met. Beyond the Basic Minimum Needs ratio, artisans identified a range of improvements they had made to their households, such as household remodeling and additions, new electronics, and various laborsaving devices. In addition, seven-point Likert-type scales with pictorial endpoints (sad face vs. happy face) similar to a scale used by Brinkerhoff, Fredell, and Frideres (1997) were used for artisans to subjectively rate their ability to provide for their families' basic needs, both currently and before starting work with MarketPlace. A more general, subjective measure of quality of life asked participants to rate their satisfaction with life both before working with MarketPlace and since working with MarketPlace. Participants responded on the seven-point Likert-type endpoints described earlier.

In addition to quantitative measures, qualitative data were also collected. Participants were asked to respond to the question, "Since you have been working with MarketPlace, what are the most important changes in your life?" Also, throughout the interviews, interviewers recorded qualitative comments made by the artisans that provided greater context to the study.

To summarize, the interviews progressed through a series of topics covering the following:

- Work history prior to and with MarketPlace

- Family membership and household composition

- MarketPlace responsibilities and time commitment

- Production capabilities and training

- Participation in SHARE programs

- Household income and expenses, diet, and housing

- Household problems, decision making, and respect

- Changes in self and other MarketPlace artisans

The format for interview questions varied. Open-ended "grand tour, example, and experience" questions (Spradley 1979) were designed to gain an insider's conceptualization of the women's lives and were carefully worded to avoid leading the informants' responses (Miles and Huberman 1994). Quantitative items related to income, family size, age, marital status, and ratings of quality of life were also included.

Interviews were carried out in Hindi. In conducting interviews, a pair of Earthwatch volunteers teamed with a hired female Indian interpreter who was a student at one of the Mumbai colleges. One Earthwatch volunteer was responsible for asking questions and offering follow-up probes in English to the interpreter. The other volunteer took notes as the interpreter provided answers. Each team of volunteers conducted two interviews per day, on average, with interviews lasting from fifty minutes to two hours and ten minutes.

In total, 161 artisans and six group leaders were interviewed between May 2001 and June 2003. Every attempt was made to interview as many members of each artisan group as possible. However, due to illness, family obligations, or travel to their natal villages, some artisans were not available at the time Earthwatch volunteers were onsite to conduct interviews. When asked, only a few artisans chose not to participate in the interviews; their wishes were honored.

Photoelicitation

For Chapter 4, a subset of twenty-six interviews was conducted through a process of photoelicitation for assessing how artisans viewed their lives and work. The photoelicitation was designed to assist us in creating a context for placing MarketPlace work within the broad array of activities that women participate in each day.

Photoelicitation, also called autophotography in psychology research or autodriving in consumer behavior studies, is a research technique whereby stimuli from the informant's environment, in this case photographs, are self ("auto") employed by the informant to "drive" an ensuing interview (Heisley and Levy 1991; Wallendorf and Belk 1987; Zeller 1990). Not only do the pictorial stimuli lead to understanding the meaning in people's lives, but the photographs can also be employed by researchers to inventory what a group values in their material culture, such as household products and decoration.

As applied to research on empowerment and quality of life, photoelicitation has been employed as a valuable field research tool to introduce informants' criteria for self-assessing their lives (Roncoli and Sendze 1997). Through photos, informants offer a voice that might not be heard in shaping how their quality of life is discussed and analyzed (Karp 1999). Forms of interpersonal connectedness, self-perceptions, and role identities often emerge in photoelicitation discussions (Dollinger and Clancy 1993). Photoelicitation can be particularly effective with illiterate or semiliterate informants (Lynd 2000), or where informants' lived experiences are dramatically different than those of the researchers (Kaufman-Scarborough 2001). Our research incorporated both circumstances.

For the photoelicitation interviews, we provided artisans with cameras and twenty-four-exposure film. We then scheduled a training session to discuss camera use. Employing a teaching strategy commonly employed at MarketPlace, we first showed one woman the details of camera use. She in turn demonstrated to the other women. Each woman was then encouraged to handle the camera and look through the viewfinder as a way of confirming that the camera was facing the right direction and her fingers were not covering the flash.

Following the camera demonstration, artisans discussed who and what they might photograph. Our guidelines or "shooting script" to the artisans were open-ended in how they chose to depict and present themselves across a typical day (English 1988). Specifically, we requested, "We want you to include pictures of your activities during the day, from when you arise in the morning until going to bed. These photos can be of anything as long as they tell something about who you are, your work, your family, and the neighborhood where you live."

After the film was processed, one set of photos was given to each woman to keep. Using a second set of photos, we asked the artisans to discuss the pictures in two ways. First, they were requested to select from the twenty-four photos a series that depicted a typical day. Artisans characteristically picked eight to ten photos for this exercise in which they identified the time of day, location, people, and activities. After discussing their typical days, the artisans next chose and further discussed two to three photos from the full set that most told about "who you are and about your life." Not uncommonly, women included a photo from the original set of twenty-four that had not been used in describing a typical day.

Twenty-six women were purposefully chosen for the photoelicitation from the four production groups located near the MarketPlace office, with variety sought in age, family situation, and life experiences. Twenty-six was the maximum number of photoelicitation interviews that could be conducted during the field research period, given the logistics of borrowing and returning cameras to the office and processing film. Photoelicitation interviews ranging from fifty minutes to two hours and ten minutes were conducted by three-person teams following the procedures described above for the other interviews.

Data Analysis

On a daily basis, Earthwatch volunteers entered quantitative data and typed narrative notes from their interviews into a laptop computer. Quantitative data were analyzed with descriptive and inferential statistics. We substituted mean values for cases with some missing household expense data. Univariate analysis of variance and chi-square analyses were employed for testing differences between two groups. Artisans who met Basic Minimum Needs with their household incomes and who earned living wages were compared with those artisans who did not achieve these income and wage goals. Paired sample t-tests were used to test differences in perceived ability to meet basic needs and satisfaction with life prior to and since coming to work for MarketPlace.

Narrative data from the interviews and the photoelicitation were analyzed in two ways. Themes from the discussion were generated using constant-comparative data analysis (Glaser and Strauss 1967; Strauss and Corbin 1990). As the discussions evolve, each new theme was compared to previous units for similarities and differences. The process of "constant comparing" leads to both continual refinement and eventual evolution toward broader conceptual insights. While we worked from an inductive approach in eliciting themes, we were also attentive to topics such as product-related associations, role behaviors, power and conflict relations, interpersonal connections, and self-perceptions that have emerged in other photoelicitation research (Dollinger and Clancy 1993; Heisley and Levy 1991). In addition, in order to identify patterns of time usage from the photoelicitation, we tracked the hour-by-hour activities in each woman's day using Microsoft Excel.

References

2009 CIA world fact book. Available at www.cia.gov/library/publications/the-world-factbook/geos/in.html.

Anokhi. 2009. *Contemporary crafted textiles.* Available at www.anokhi.com/anokhi/about-us.html.

Asia Floor Wage Alliance Campaign. 2009. *Stitching a decent wage across borders.* Available at www.asiafloorwage.org.

Askerud, P., and Englehardt, R. 2007. *Statistics on cultural industries: Framework for the elaboration of national data capacity building projects.* Bangkok: UNESCO Bangkok.

Basu, K. 1995. Marketing developing society crafts. A framework for analysis and change. In J. A. Costa and G. J. Bamossy (Eds.), *Marketing in a multicultural world*, 257-298. Thousand Oaks, CA: Sage.

Bhatt, E. R. 2006. *We are poor but so many: The story of self-employed women in India.* Oxford, UK: Oxford University Press.

Bhatt, E. R. 2008, September 25. *What do poor and women want to come out of poverty?* Speech given to the United Nations General Assembly. Available at www.sewa.org/Press-Note.asp.

Biswas-Diener, R., and Diener, E. 2001. Making the best of a bad situation in the slums of Calcutta. *Social Indicators Research, 55:* 329-352.

Bremer, M. 2002. *Defining and measuring a global living wage: Theoretical and conceptual issues.* Available at www.umass.edu/peri.

Brinkerhoff, M. B., Fredell, K. A., and Frideres, J. S. 1997. Basic minimum needs, quality of life, and selected correlates: Explorations in villages in Northern India. *Social Indicators Research*, 42: 245-281.

Business for Social Responsibility. 2002. *Wages—Living wage.* Available at www.bsr.org.

Center for Reflection, Education and Action. n.d. *Sustainable living wages and income.* Available at http://www.crea-inc.org/.

Chambers, R. 1997. *Whose reality counts? Putting the first last.* London: Intermediate Technology Publications.

Chatterjee, A. 2007, Fall. Craft crisis in India. *Hand/Eye: The Aid to Artisans Magazine*, 12.

Clarkson, M. B. E. 1995. A stakeholder framework for analyzing and evaluating corporate social performance. *The Academy of Management Review*, 20, no. 1: 92-117.

Cockram, M. 2005. *Lessons learned in twenty years: Honduras, Ghana, Hungary, Russia, Armenia, Central Asia, and Peru.* Hartford, CT: Aid to Artisans.

Cone Communications Press Release. 2006. *The 2004 Cone Corporate Citizenship Study.* Available at www.coneinc.com/research/archive.php.

Conroy, M. E. 2007. *Branded! How the "certification revolution" is transforming global corporations.* Gabriola Island, British Columbia: New Society Publisher.

Dana, L. P. 2000. Creating entrepreneurs in India. *Journal of Small Business Management*, 38, no. 1: 86-91.

de Certeau, M. 1984. *The practice of everyday life.* Berkeley: University of California Press.

Dhamija, J. 1989. Women and handcrafts: Myth and reality. In E. Leonard (Ed.), *Seeds: Supporting women's work in the Third World*, 195-211. New York: Feminist Press.

Dickson, M. A. 2005. Identifying and profiling apparel label users. In R. Harrison, T. Newholm, and D. Shaw (Eds.), *The ethical consumer*, 155-172. London: Sage.

Dickson, M. A., and Kovaleski, K. 2007, November 8. *Implementing labor compliance in the apparel industry* (poster). International Textiles and Apparel Association. Los Angeles, CA.

Dickson, M. A., Loker, S., and Eckman, M. 2009. *Social responsibility in the global apparel industry.* New York: Fairchild Books.

Dollinger, S. J., and Clancy, S. M. 1993. Identity, self, and personality: II. Glimpses through the autophotographic eye. *Journal of Personality and Social Psychology*, 64, no. 6: 1064-1071.

Durham, D. E., and Littrell, M. A. 2000. Performance factors of Peace Corps handcraft enterprises as indicators of income generation and sustainability. *Clothing and Textiles Research Journal*, 18, no. 4: 260-272.

Earthwatch Fact Sheet. 2009. Available at www.earthwatch.org/newsandevents/presskit/earthwatch_fact_sheet.

English, F. W. 1988. The utility of the camera in qualitative inquiry. *Educational Research*, 47, no. 4: 8-15.

European Fair Trade Association. 2008. Available at http://www.european-fair-trade-association.org.

Fairtrade Labelling Organization (FLO). n.d. *Products.* Available at http://www.fairtrade.net/products.html.

Fairtrade Labelling Organization (FLO). n.d. *Aims of fair trade standards.* Available at http://www.fairtrade.net/aims_of_fairtrade_standards.html.

Frater, J. 2002, September. *Contemporary embroideries of Rabaris of Kutch: Economic and cultural viability.* Paper presented at the Eighth Biennial Symposium of the Textile Society of America. Smith College, North Hampton, MA.

Fridell, G. 2007. *Fair trade coffee: The prospects and pitfalls of market-driven social justice.* Toronto, Ontario, Canada: University of Toronto Press.

Fridell, G. 2009. The co-operative and the corporation: Competing visions of the future of fair trade. *Journal of Business Ethics*, 86, supplement 1: 81-95.

Glaser, B. G., and Strauss, A. 1967. *The discovery of grounded theory: Strategies for qualitative research.* Chicago: Aldine.

Gogoi, P. 2008, June 18. Is fair trade becoming 'fair trade lite'? *BusinessWeek.* Available at http://www.businessweek.com.

Gottschling, B., Littrell, M. A., and Cockram, M. 2005. *An artisan association is born: A case study of Aid to Artisans in Central Asia., 1994-1999.* Hartford, CT: Aid to Artisans.

Green, N. L. 2003. Fashion, flexible specialization, and the sweatshop: A historical problem. In D. E. Bender and R. A. Greenwald (Eds.), *Sweatshop USA: The American sweatshop in historical and global perspective*, 37-56. New York: Routledge.

Grimes, K. M., and Milgram, B. L. (Eds.). 2000. *Artisans and cooperatives: Developing alternative trade for the global economy.* Tucson: University of Arizona Press.

Guyer, J. L., Denzer, L., and Agbaje, A. (Eds.). 2002. *Money struggles and city life: Devaluation in Ibadan and other urban centers in southern Nigeria, 1986-1996.* Portsmouth, NH: Heinemann.

Handy, F., Kassam, M., Feeney, S., and Ranade, B. 2006. *Grass-roots NGOs by women for women: The driving force of development in India.* Thousand Oaks, CA: Sage.

Heisley, D. D., and Levy, S. J. 1991. Autodriving: A photoelicitation technique. *Journal of Consumer Research*, 18, no. 3: 257-272.

Hill, E. 2001. Women in the Indian informal economy: Collective strategies for work life improvement and development. *Work, Employment and Society*, 15: 443-464.

Hira, A., and Ferrie, J. 2006. Fair trade: Three key challenges for reaching the mainstream. *Journal of Business Ethics*, 63: 107-118.

Honneth, A. 1995. *The struggle for recognition.* Cambridge, UK: Polity Press.

Human development report 2009. Retrieved from http://hdrstats. undp.org/en/countries/country_fact_sheets/cty_fs_IND.html

Hurley, J. 2005. Unravelling the web: Supply chains and workers' lives in the garment industry. In A. Hale and J. Willis (Eds.), *Threads of labour: Garment industry supply chains from the workers' perspective*, 95-132. Malden, MA: Blackwell Publishing.

International Labour Organization (ILO). 2007. *Toolkit for mainstreaming employment and decent work* (2nd ed.). Geneva: ILO. Available at http://www.ilo.org/public/english/bureau/dgo/selecdoc/2007/toolkit. pdf.

International Labour Organization (ILO). n.d. *Decent work for all*. Available at http://www.ilo.org/global/About_the_ILO/Mainpillars/ WhatisDecentWork/lang-en/index.htm.

Joshi, T. 2001. *Significance of the crafts sector in India.* Crafts Workshop: India.

Kala Raksha Vidhyalaya: An institution of design for traditional artisans. 2009. Available at www.kala-raksha.org/vidhyalaya.htm.

Karp, D. A. 1999. Social science, progress, and the ethnographer's craft. *Journal of Contemporary Ethnography*, 28, no. 6: 597-609.

Kaufman-Scarborough, C. 2001. Sharing the experience of mobility-disabled consumers: Building understanding through the use of ethnographic research methods. *Journal of Contemporary Ethnography*, 30, no. 4: 430-464.

Keahey, J., Littrell, M. A., and Murray, D. L. Forthcoming. Business with a mission: The ongoing role of Ten Thousand Villages within the fair trade movement. In A. E. Weaver (Ed.), *A table of sharing: Mennonite Central Committee and the expanding networks of Mennonite identity.* Telford, PA: Cascadia Publishing.

Korten, D. C. 1987. Third generation NGO strategies: A key to people-centered development. *World Development*, 15, supplement 1: 145-159.

Krier, J. 2007. *Fair trade 2007: New facts and figures from an ongoing success story.* Available at www.wfto.com/index.php?option=com_docmanandtask=cat_viewandgrid=94andandItemid=109.

Layton, R. 2004. Enhancing intellectual property exports through fair trade. In J. M. Finger and P Schuler (Eds.), *Poor people's knowledge: Intellectual property in developing countries*, 75-93. Washington, DC: World Bank and Oxford University Press.

Liebl, M. 2005, February 22-26. *Jodhpur: The most creative of communities.* Paper presented at the Conference on Asia-Pacific Creative Communities: A Strategy for the 21st Century Senior Expert Symposium, Jodhpur, India. Available at: www.unescobkk.org/fileadmin/user_upload/culture/ Cultural Industries/presentations/Opening_Session_-_Maureen Liebl. pdf.

Liebl, M., and Roy, T. 2001. *Summary of main conclusions related to project goals.* Crafts Workshop: India. Available at http://lnweb18. worldbank.org.

Liebl, M., and Roy, T. 2003. Handmade in India: Preliminary analysis of crafts producers and crafts production. *Economic and Political Weekly*, 38, no. 51/52: 5366-5376.

Liebl, M., and Roy, T. 2004. Handmade in India: Traditional craft skills in a changing world. In J. M. Finger and P. Schuler (Eds.), *Poor people's knowledge: Intellectual property in developing countries*, 53-73. Washington, DC: World Bank and Oxford University Press.

Lindholm, H. 2009, October 26. *The Jo-In multi-stakeholders' approach: Lessons for wage issues.* Presentation at the Fair Labor Association's conference on Wages Along the Supply Chain: Assessment and Prospects, Washington, DC.

Littrell, M. A., and Dickson, M. A. 1999. *Social responsibility in the global market: Fair trade of cultural products.* Thousand Oaks, CA: Sage.

Littrell, M. A., Cockram, M., and Strawn, S. 2005a. *Entrepreneurship and cultural passion: A case study of Aid to Artisans in Armenia.* Hartford, CT: Aid to Artisans.

Littrell, M. A., Cockram, M., and Strawn, S. 2005b. *A rich and deeply cultural tradition: A case study of Aid to Artisans in Ghana.* Hartford, CT: Aid to Artisans.

Littrell, M. A., Ma, Y. J., and Halepete, J. 2005. Generation X, baby boomers, and swing: Marketing fair trade apparel. *Journal of Fashion Marketing and Management*, 9, no. 4: 407-419.

Luce, E. 2007. *In spite of the gods: The strange rise of modern India.* New York: Doubleday.

Lynd, M. 2000. The international craft market: A double-edged sword for Guatemalan Maya women. In K. M. Grimes and B. L. Milgram (Eds.), *Artisans and cooperatives: Developing alternative trade for the global economy,* 65-83. Tucson: University of Arizona Press.

MacHenry, R. 2000. Building on local strengths: Nepalese fair trade textiles. In K. M. Grimes and B. L. Milgram (Eds.), *Artisans and cooperatives: Developing alternative trade for the global economy,* 25-44. Tucson: University of Arizona Press.

Maquila Solidarity Network (MSN). 2006. *Is fair trade a good fit for the garment industry?* Available at http://en.maquilasolidarity.org/node/215?SESS89c5db41a82abcd7da7c9ac60e04ca5f =am9d2mcaam5g8enk2ah q0oo5r1.

Miles, M. B., and Huberman, A. M. 1994. *Qualitative data analysis.* Thousand Oaks, CA: Sage.

Milgram, B. L. 2000. Reorganizing textile production for the global market. In K. M. Grimes and B. L. Milgram (Eds.), *Artisans and cooperatives: Developing alternative trade for the global economy,* 107-128. Tucson: University of Arizona Press.

Misha Black Award. 2009. Available at www.mishablackawards.org.uk/pages/2009_med_frater.htm.

Morris, W. F., Jr. 1996. *Handmade money: Latin American artisans in the marketplace.* Washington, DC: Organization of American States.

Mukherjee, A., and Reed, D. 2009. Fair trade and development: What are the implications of mainstreaming? *Universitas Forum,* 1, no. 2: 1-8.

Mukherjee, R. 1981. On the quality of life in India: An exploratory survey. *Social Indicators Research,* 9: 455-476.

Murray, D. L., and Raynolds, L. T. 2007. Globalization and its antimonies: Negotiating a fair trade movement. In L. T. Raynolds, D. L Murray, and J. Wilkinson (Eds.), *Fair trade: The challenges of transforming globalization,* 3-14. New York, NY: Routledge.

Murray, D. L., Raynolds, L. T., and Taylor, P. L. 2003. *Poverty alleviation and fair trade coffee in Latin America.* Fort Collins, CO: Colorado State University Fair Trade Research Group.

Nash, J. 2000. Postscript: To market, to market. In K. M. Grimes and B. L. Milgram (Eds.), *Artisans and cooperatives: Developing alternative trade for the global economy,* 175-179. Tucson: University of Arizona Press.

Nicholls, A., and Opal, C. 2005. *Fair trade: Market driven ethical consumption*. London: Sage.

Nussbaum, M. 2000. *Women and human development: The capabilities approach*. Cambridge, UK: Cambridge University Press.

Nussbaum, M., and Sen, A. (Eds.). 1993. *The quality of life*. Oxford, UK: Carendon.

Office of the United Nations High Commissioner for Human Rights. 2006. *Frequently asked questions on a human rights-based approach to development cooperation*. New York: United Nations. Available at http://www.ohchr.org/Documents/Publications/FAQen.pdf.

Okafor, F. C. 1985. Basic needs in rural Nigeria. *Social Indicators Research*, 17: 115-125.

Paige-Reeves, J. 1998. Alpaca sweater design and marketing: Problems and prospects for cooperative knitting organizations in Bolivia. *Human Organization*, 57, no. 1: 83-93.

Porter, M. S., and Kramer, M. R. 2006. Strategy and society: The link between competitive advantage and corporate social responsibility. *Harvard Business Review*, 84, no. 12: 78-92.

Quigley, M., and Opal, C. 2006. *Fair trade garment standards: Feasibility study completed for Transfair USA*. Available at http://www.transfairusa.org/pdfs/FT%20Garment%20Standards%20Feasibility%20Study.pdf.

Radhakrishnan, S. 2003, December 15. A truly Anokhi story. *The Hindu Business Line*. Available at www.thehindubusinessline.com/life/2003/12/15/stories/2003121500020100.htm.

Raynolds, L. T., and Wilkinson, J. 2007. Fair trade in the agriculture and food sector: Analytical dimensions. In L. T. Raynolds, D. L Murray, and J. Wilkinson (Eds.), *Fair trade: The challenges of transforming globalization*, 33-47. New York, NY: Routledge.

Reed, D. 2009. What do corporations have to do with fair trade? Positive and normative analysis from a value chain perspective. *Journal of Business Ethics*, 86, supplement 1: 3-26.

Renard, M. 2005. Quality certification, regulation and power in fair trade. *Journal of Rural Studies*, 21, no. 4: 419-431.

Robinson, I., and Athreya, B. 2005, March 22. *Constructing markets for conscientious apparel consumers: Adapting the "fair trade" model to the apparel sector*. Background paper prepared for the Conference on Constructing Markets for Conscientious Apparel Consumers, University of Michigan–Ann Arbor, April 1-2.

Roncoli, C., and Sendze, M. 1997. Visions and voices of Donsin: How farmers of Burkina Faso participate as photographers. *Practicing Anthropology*, 19, no. 3: 26-30.

Rosenbaum, B. 2000. Of women, hope, and angels: Fair trade and artisan production in a squatter settlement in Guatemala City. In K. M. Grimes and B. L. Milgram (Eds.), *Artisans and cooperatives: Developing alternative trade for the global economy,* 85-106. Tucson: University of Arizona Press.

Rosenbaum, B., and Goldin, L. 1997. New exchange processes in the international market: The re-making of Maya artisan production in Guatemala. *Museum Anthropology*, 21, no. 2: 72-82.

Roy, T. 2001. *Overview of the economics of the crafts industries.* Crafts Workshop: India. Available at http://lnweb18.worldbank.org.

Sen, A. 1980. Equality of what? In S. McMurrin (Ed.), *The Tanner lectures on human values: I.* Cambridge, UK: Cambridge University Press.

Sen, A. 1993. Capability and well-being. In M. Nussbaum and A. Sen (Eds.), *The quality of life,* 30-52. Oxford, UK: Carendon.

Shaw, D., and Shiu, E. 2002. The role of ethical obligation and self-identity in ethical consumer choice. *International Journal of Consumer Studies*, 26, no. 2: 109-116.

Silverman, E. 2009, October 26. *The Fair Wage Guide for crafts artisans: Method and achievements.* Presentation at the Fair Labor Association's conference on Wages Along the Supply Chain: Assessment and Prospects, Washington, DC.

Smith, S., and Barrientos, S. 2005. Fair trade and ethical trade: Are there moves towards convergence? *Sustainable Development*, 13: 190-198.

Spradley, J. P. 1979. *The ethnographic interview.* New York: Holt, Rinehart and Winston.

Srinivas, A. 2008, July 14. *Starvation threat looms as food, fuel prices shoot up.* www.Sify.com.

Stephen, L. 1991. Culture as a resource: Four cases of self-managed indigenous craft production in Latin America. *Economic Development and Cultural Change*, 40, no. 1: 101-130.

Strauss, A., and Corbin, J. 1990. *Basics of qualitative research.* Newbury Park, CA: Sage.

Strawn, S., and Littrell, M. A. 2006. Beyond capabilities: A case study of three artisan enterprises in India. *Clothing and Textiles Research Journal*, 24, no. 3: 207-213.

Tallontire, A., Rentsendorj, E., and Blowfield, M. 2001. *Ethical consumers and ethical trade: A review of current literature.* Kent, UK: Natural Resources Institute of the University of Greenwich.

Thompson, E. P. 1978. *The poverty of theory.* London: Merlin Press.

Tice, K. 1995. *Kuna crafts, gender, and the global economy.* Austin: University of Texas Press.

Traill, W. B. 1999, October 11-15. *Prospects for the future: Nutritional, environmental and sustainable food production considerations—Changes in cultural and consumer habits.* Presented at the UK Conference on International Food Trade Beyond 2000: Science-Based Decisions, Harmonization, Equivalence and Mutual Recognition, Melbourne, Australia. Available at http://www.fao.org/docrep/meeting/X2697e.htm.

Transfair USA. *Apparel Products.* Available at http://transfairusa.org/content/certification/apparel_program.php.

Transfair USA. 2009, November. Pilot Program for Fair Trade Certified Apparel & Home Goods: Obligations of CMT Facilities, ver. 2. Available at http://www.transfairusa.org/content/Downloads/garments.pdf.

Turner, S. 2007. Trading old textiles: The selective diversification of highland livelihoods in Northern Vietnam. *Human Organization*, 66, no. 4: 389-425.

US Department of Labor. 2000. *Wages, benefits, poverty line, and meeting workers' needs in the apparel and footwear industries of selected countries.* Washington, DC: Author.

Vaughan-Whitehead, D. 2009. *Incorporating "fair wages" into CSR.* Paper presented at the Fair Labor Association's conference on Wages Along the Supply Chain: Assessment and Prospects, Washington, DC.

Wallendorf, M., and Belk, R. W. 1987. *Deep meaning in possessions: Qualitative research from the consumer behavior odyssey* (videotape). Cambridge, MA: Marketing Science Institute.

WFTO. 2009. *SFTMS: Sustainable fair trade management system, draft two.* Available at http://www.wfto.com/

WFTO. 2009. *Frequently asked questions.* Available at http://www.wfto.com/

WFTO. 2009. *Marks and labels.* Available at http://www.wfto.com/

WFTO. 2009. *Monitoring.* Available at http://www.wfto.com/

WFTO. 2009. *Ten standards of fair trade.* Available at http://www.wfto.com/

WFTO. 2009. *The World Fair Trade Organization.* Available at http://www.wfto.com/

Wilkinson-Weber, C. M. 1999. *Embroidering lives: Women's work and skill in the Lucknow embroidery industry.* Albany, NY: State University of New York Press.

Zeller, R. C. 1990. *Photographing the self: Methods for observing personal orientations.* Newbury Park, CA: Sage.

About the Authors

Dr. Mary A. Littrell is Professor and Department Head in Design and Merchandising at Colorado State University. She received her Ph.D. from Purdue University. Dr. Littrell's research addresses multiple facets of business social responsibility, with special focus on artisan enterprises. Across her internationally recognized work, she has examined how textile artisan enterprises achieve viability in the increasingly competitive global market for artisan products. Dr. Littrell's research has taken her around the world in illuminating the lives of textile artisans and the challenges they face in the global market, culminating in her first book *Social Responsibility in the Global Market: Fair Trade of Cultural Products* with coauthor Dr. Marsha A. Dickson. In recognition of their previous research and their work in India, the coauthors were named Rockefeller Center Scholars in Bellagio, Italy. Additional published research includes an edited book, eight book chapters, and over sixty journal articles. Dr. Littrell serves as Associate Editor for *Textile: The Journal of Cloth and Culture* and is on the Editorial Board of the *Journal of Fashion Marketing and Management*. She is a *Fellow* of the International Textile and Apparel Association and of the Society for Applied Anthropology.

Dr. Marsha A. Dickson is Professor and Department Chairperson in Fashion and Apparel Studies at the University of Delaware. Her Ph.D. was earned at Iowa State University. Dr. Dickson is internationally known for her research and teaching on socially responsible practices in the apparel industry. Her research has been conducted in several countries, including China, Guatemala, India, Thailand, and Vietnam. She has published with Fairchild Books a textbook, *Social Responsibility in the Global Apparel Industry*, that provides in-depth understanding of the ways that apparel brands and retailers are attempting to improve labor standards, human rights, and environmental sustainability in the apparel industry. Dr. Dickson is founder and President of an international consortium of Educators for Socially Responsible Apparel Business, whose initial membership includes over eighty apparel and textile educators from thirty-five states in the United States and seven countries. Dr. Dickson is also a member of the board of directors of the Fair Labor Association (FLA), a nongovernmental organization (NGO) originally formed by President Clinton to address labor standards and working conditions in the apparel industry. In 2009, Dr. Dickson was recognized for her academic contributions with the All Star Award from Apparel Magazine and the International Textile and Apparel Association.

Index

Also from Kumarian Press...

Globalization:

The Hidden Assembly Line: Gender Dynamics of Subcontracted
Work in a Global Economy
Edited by Radhika Balakrishnan

Southern Exposure: International Development and the Global
South in the Twenty-First Century
Barbara P. Thomas-Slayter

Development and the Private Sector: Consuming Interests
Edited by Deborah Eade and John Sayer

Women and the Politics of Place
Edited by Wendy Harcourt and Arturo Escobar

New and Forthcoming:

Rethinking Corporate Social Engagement: Lessons from Latin America
Lester M. Salamon

Dispossessed People: Establishing Legitimacy and Rights for Global Migrants
Christine Ho and James Loucky

Financial Promise for the Poor: How Groups Build Microsavings
Edited by Kim Wilson, Malcolm Harper and Matthew Griffith

Just Give Money to the Poor: The Development Revolution from the Global South
Joseph Hanlon, Armando Barrientos and David Hulme

Visit Kumarian Press at **www.kpbooks.com** or
call **toll-free 800.232.0223** for a complete catalog.

green press
INITIATIVE

 Kumarian Press, located in Sterling, Virginia, is a forward-looking, scholarly press that promotes active international engagement and an awareness of global connectedness.